Via

Adorations,

Via

Obliquities

By Philip Hughes-Luing

ISBN 979-8-9935425-3-9

Foreword

Blessed In Love

Stephen and I had a long conversation this evening as we sat in the front room looking at his memorial painting. I sat on the sofa, and he sat in a side chair, inhabiting the photo of him standing in front of the Golden Gate Bridge that had been displayed on an easel at his funeral. He pointed out to me how remarkably blessed I've been to know an unbroken flow of romantic love in my life for the past forty-some years.

Back when I was sixteen years old, Ben and I committed to be together for the rest of our lives. The week before my seventeen birthday we'd made plans to go to the same college, to the same law school, to form a law firm together, to get married and buy homes next to each other – though in retrospect I expect that eventually we would have realized that we just wanted to buy one house and get married to each other. That wasn't a concept which had yet dawned on us as a possibility in our rural northern Minnesota of 1973. In any case, a few days later Ben pulled out onto the road in front of an oncoming semi tractor-trailer, and on my seventeenth birthday I served as a pall bearer at his funeral. I made it halfway down the aisle to view him in his casket when I was paralyzed with grief and an unstaunched flow of tears. After an eternity of standing there and weeping, his mother finally came up to me, put her hands on my shoulders, and said, "It was painless." That was enough to break the spell and allow me to proceed up the aisle to view him, then go to my seat.

Upon our return home, I cut a weathered log into three lengths and worked for weeks with a hammer and chisel to hollow out spaces for three flowerpots. Ben was gone, but the commitment we made to live our lives together was not broken because to this day my love for him remains deeply rooted.

In 1979, my senior year of college, I met Dennis, and upon graduation I moved in with him. We relocated together to Portland, Oregon and then to Chicago, where he became more and more heavily involved with party drugs and heavy drinking. After two and a half years together, he asked me to move out so as not to be a part of his addiction. I did, but my love for him did not end, nor did his love for me. He kept me in his life as a touchstone with whom he'd reconnect every year or so, whenever he'd make another attempt at sobriety.

In 1982 I met Jeff, and we started our life together, but six years later, when Dennis was discharged from the AIDS ward at St. Joseph's Hospital, Jeff made room for him to stay in our extra bedroom for a year and a half as he recuperated. My love for Jeff grew immensely as he honored my commitment to be a caregiver for Dennis, then his medical power of attorney, and in 1990 to be the executor of his estate.

Shortly after Dennis died, Jeff began developing symptoms of HIV encephalopathy, and in 1994 he succumbed. I grieved for four years before starting to date again. I attended Columbia College of Chicago and was beginning to work on a book of writings for Jeff for my eventual master's thesis when, in 1998, I met Stephen.

For two years Stephen made room in our new relationship and encouraged me as I completed and self-published my book for Jeff. Stephen's support for my project honoring Jeff made permanent my love for and commitment to him. My fifteen years with Stephen were truly, as I entitled the book I gave to him as a marriage proposal, <u>Bliss</u>. We'd planned to be married here in Chicago as soon as the law legalizing same-sex marriages got through the Illinois legislature, but it stalled.

As it happened, however, for Christmas of 2012 we'd asked Stephen's mother to join us on a trip to San Francisco the following summer. When in June of 2013, proposition 8 fell, we immediately went on-line and made reservations to be married in San Francisco's City Hall the last week of July, with his mom as our witness.

In March or April of 2013, Stephen began developing an intermittent, mild pain in his side. He attributed it to using too much weight for his workouts at the gym. By the week of our wedding in July, however, the pain had become persistent and bothersome, so he called his doctor back here in Chicago. She suggested it might be an ulcer or gall bladder disease and scheduled him for an ultrasound the first week in August.

The ultrasound revealed a 17cm x 15cm x 5cm tumor on his liver which had developed from undetected, untreated hepatitis B, and which was now stage four cancerous. I was able to work from home and care for him from August through October, then took full FMLA leave in November. He died peacefully in our bed on November 15th, a day after our 15-year anniversary and three days short of his fiftieth birthday.

So now Stephen, too, has passed away, but as he pointed out as we conversed this evening, I cannot think of his death as a tragedy because at no time did our love diminish or die. While it's adjusting to new circumstances and has taken on new means of expression, it still flows strong. The love that I first knew at age sixteen with Ben has successively grown and merged with new streams of feelings for Dennis, Jeff and now Stephen. While I've experienced the death of four men whom I loved, with whom I committed to share my life, I've never experienced the death of love. I realize that is a rare thing to be able to say, and in that I feel extremely blessed. For that I am extremely grateful.

The above passage was written on 12-21-2013

The following collection is drawn from my writings that span a period of over fifty years, from 1974 until the present, mostly written for an audience of one, pieces written for and about these four men.

I.   Via Adorations

Contents

Illustrations:

I. <u>Via Adorations</u>

Book 1 — *First Loves*

<u>Chapter 1 — *Ben*</u>

**On the night of July 4, 1974, going into
the next morning, I wrote the following:**

Seventeen

Dear Lord,

Tomorrow, in but a few hours,
 it will be Friday and my seventeenth birthday.
 I don't want to be seventeen, because when I'm seventeen
 I must carry my closest friend out to a hole in the ground.
 Oh Lord, please spare me my seventeenth year.

It would seem so good to remain sixteen. Last Saturday,
 when I was sixteen, I saw Ben. We talked.
 Communication, even through silence, is so free
 when time is only the present, and a lifelong friendship
 is thought of as being in decades.

We – Ben, his brother Dan, and I – went fishing
 that afternoon, and we laughed as I tried
 to back the boat trailer to the lake in a straight line,
 and we laughed when we forgot to unstrap the boat
 from the trailer, and we joked about the huge size
 of the fish we caught, and we found the bit of humor

in the motor that flooded, causing us to wade along shore,
pulling our floating tub, and we cheered when Ben
persuaded the motor to start again, and all was done
in the deepest sense of friendship.

The Tuesday after that, when I was still sixteen,
I received a letter from Ben with plans for us
to be counselors together at a summer Bible camp
the following week. Tuesday evening
a long-distance phone call
telling of a car and grain-truck collision came.
Camping plans were cancelled. Sweet Sixteen turned sour.

Lord, perhaps tomorrow when it is Friday and my birthday,
I should be eighteen. Time is said to be the healer of sorrows.
Perhaps a year could at least mellow the grief.
If life must go on, dear Lord, let mine go on from eighteen.

Excuse me, Lord, the sun has risen, and it's Friday,
and it's my birthday, and I'm seventeen. I must go walk
with my closest friend, only this time he won't walk, or talk,
or laugh or jest, and the silence will carry
but one-way communication.
Seventeen feels like a very old age,
a lifetime old.

Our Correspondence

**Ben was either the last traumatic stress
of my childhood, or my first as an adult.**

On the way to the funeral my mother chided me
 for worrying too much about which bow tie to wear,
 because nobody would be thinking about me.

On the way home she again chided me
 for having made a spectacle of myself
 and having embarrassed the whole family
 by stopping and standing, paralyzed, immobile,
 halfway down the aisle to view the body,
 weeping uncontrollably until finally
 the spell was broken by Ben's mother,
 who shouldn't have had to be thinking about me
 at such a time, putting her arms around my shoulders
 and whispering, "It was painless, instantaneous."
 She was a schoolteacher.

Ben and I had made a game of exchanging letters:
 sentences playfully written in spirals or backwards,
 or from the bottom of the page to the top, right to left,
 his interspersed with creative spellings, which later
 I would realize were products of dyslexia, but at the time
 were just additional puzzles for me to solve, engagements
 to bring our minds closer together, games we played
 at a distance of one hundred miles, my family having moved
 from the town where we met, where he lived, where his eyes
 had sparkled, and wide grins had spread across his freckled,

Dutch-Germanic, wide-featured, farm-boy face
whenever we got together, usually at church or at his home,
with his younger brother, Dan.

Ben's smile melted my otherness, the warmth
of his generous spirit focused on me, wrapping us in joy
as we shared recipes to try out or exchanged patterns
for sewing our own hand-tied, oversized bow ties,
often in jumbo plaids, a fashion trend in the early Seventies.

Just the weekend before, prior to my seventeenth birthday,
Ben and his family had visited us. Ben, Dan, and I fished
and spoke of our futures. Dan didn't want college, instead
he wanted to be a farmer, to work with his hands, grow crops,
raise farm animals. Ben and I wanted to be lawyers,
made plans to go to the same college, same law school,
together to open a law firm, to get married,
perhaps in a double ceremony to as-yet-unknown women,
perhaps sisters, to buy homes next to each other's,
in short, to spend the rest of our lives with each other.

Sex, of course, wasn't mentioned, being a taboo topic,
just how much fun we could have being counselors
together at a children's Bible camp later that month.
I didn't disclose to Ben and Dan that I had rebelled
in my thinking, wanted to have friends more
than respect, had decided that I couldn't believe
that out of all the people who had lived throughout
the world, throughout history, only real, born-again
Christians, such a minute portion, could be redeemed,
awarded resurrection into eternal glory, while everyone else,

the ninety-nine point nine, nine, nine ad infinitum percent
of humanity would perish, would burn eternally
in a lake of fire. Swallowing my inner doubts, wanting
more time with Ben, I agreed to be a Bible-camp counselor.

I didn't know I was gay, didn't even know what the word
homosexual meant, didn't know that gay sex was possible,
had never imagined, until I saw a play during my junior year
of college, one which made what I had felt for Ben
make sense, explained how, on my seventeenth birthday,
when our law firm had been dissolved, what I had
experienced had been my first loss of an entire lifetime.

Was this God's punishment for my wanting friends,
for being willing to break rules and drink cans of beer
in cornfields after baseball games?

For the next year I was volatile, exploding in fits
of rage, particularly at my mother, who'd told me
that I was meant to be an evangelist like Billy Graham,
that I should use my scholarship to attend Bethel College,
Wheaton College, or Moody Bible Institute.

Sometimes in the middle of the night, I would quietly knock
on my parents' bedroom door and ask them to forgive me,
or to tell them that I forgave them, depending
on my state of mind. In either case, the silence
was always the same, except for once my father told me
that I needed to ask God, not them, to forgive me.

<u>Chapter 2 – *Interlude*</u>

Deliver Us, O Lord
(autofiction)

"Why am I doing this?"

The question pressed out in all directions
from the very center of Robert's brain.

He kept his mouth closed, his lips thin and tight.
He gripped the steering wheel of the car
with both of his hands as he drove north on the freeway
into the dark, northern Minnesota night.

The road was wet. A fog had been hanging in the air
all day. He held the car to a steady 55 miles per hour.
The windshield wipers beat back and forth slowly,
leaving a streak across his field of vision.
He'd been meaning to replace them for some time,
but usually only thought of it when rain fell.
There were always so many chores waiting to be done
around the house and out in the barn, plus a full-time job
at the paper mill. He was a superintendent there
in the machine room, so he was always on call.

He'd made this twenty-mile trip up to Cloquet many a time
in the middle of the night when someone had called
to say that one of the machines was down. But tonight
he wasn't headed for the paper mill.

They rode along in silence. Neither of them
felt like turning on the radio. It wasn't a night for music.

Each knew that whatever station one of them would choose
the other wouldn't like anyway, so they settled for listening
to the steady beat of the wipers and the sound
of each other breathing. Neither had spoken a word
since getting into the car. It wasn't a night for talk, either.

"Raise up a child in the way of the Lord, and when he is grown
he will not depart far from it." Robert repeated this to himself
silently. This was the counsel their pastor had given them
when he and Faith had gone to see him to confide in him
that their son had fallen into this sin.

The pastor had said it wasn't unusual for young men
to go through a period of rebellion against their parents
and against God, and that their best weapon
against Satan's hold on their son was to steady themselves
with prayer and to remain steadfast in their belief
that their son would find his way back to God's Word.
"Let him go, and he'll soon see the error of his ways."

Philip Dean. He and his older sister, Phyllis Jean,
named after dear friends, Dean and Jean, whom he and Faith
had supported in their missionary work, Evangelical Free
Christians in the Philippines. They had passed

away years ago. How heartbroken they would be if they knew how this child named for them had been taken by the Devil.

Robert swallowed hard and cleared his throat. His son turned, looked, afraid that he was going to say something, but he didn't. He just kept staring ahead at the road, driving them through the tunnel of shadowy outlines of tall pine trees rising on either side. Philip turned his own gaze back to the road ahead of them.

"Yes, Pastor, let him go," Robert thought, "but to deliver him directly into the hands of evil?" Robert clenched. He gripped the steering wheel tighter, thinking of their destination. "We did let him go, we let him go to that college with no religious affiliation whatsoever, down in the south of Iowa, too far away for us to even visit.

"And on a full scholarship from the paper mill! Only eligible for it because I spent the last twenty years working there. God gave him the gift of a college education anywhere he chooses, and he chooses to throw it back in God's face!"

Robert grimaced as he remembered their embarrassment when they'd read in their local paper about their son having a part in the play "Gypsy", a musical comedy celebrating the life of a notorious burlesque stripper. They'd called him about that. It was the last time they'd seen anything from their son's college in the paper.

But the trouble hadn't started in college. Faith had said there were times when Philip would break into rages, scream at her at the top of his lungs, say that he hated them,

couldn't stand living with them, then storm out of the house.
Late at night he'd come and knock on their bedroom door,
say he was sorry, that he really loved them. They knew
he was struggling with something but had no idea what.

All they could think to do was to tell him to go back to bed,
to ask God for His forgiveness. "How was I to have handled
this rebellion?" Robert asked himself. "Should I have
threatened him that if he didn't show more respect
for his mother that I'd, what?"

Robert felt his face flushing with anger. His stomach ached.
He stretched the back of his neck and shoulders, swallowed
again. Robert thought of his own rebellion of sorts
when he was in the army over in Korea, where he'd served
as a radio engineer. He'd gotten tired of the taunts
of fellow recruits calling him Mr. Upright and Uptight
so he'd begun smoking a few cigarettes with the guys
to try to fit in. It wasn't long before he was asking God
to forgive him, but by then it was too late. He was hooked.
It wasn't until he'd gotten back to the States that Faith
had put an end to this vice, as a condition of their marriage.

Robert flinched. How likely was his son to find someone
like Faith if he kept on living the kind of life he was pursuing?
A picture of his son flashed through his mind. He closed
his eyes to suppress it. Faith. How tender, how holy
it was to make love with her. Afterwards it always felt
like they'd been joined in prayer. And God had blessed them
with nine children, all healthy, each gifted in their own way.

Now here was his eldest son, defiling God's gift of the love
shared between a man and a woman, a husband and a wife.
And here he was, driving his son up to meet with someone
he was sure was one of those deviants. He felt a sickness
in his stomach, had to clear his throat again.

"How had his son come to this perversion? How much
of this is my own fault?" Robert wondered. He'd never
had a lot of time to spend doing things with his son.
They'd taken that hiking trip with the church's youth group.
He'd taken him deer hunting every season. But his son
was a loner, didn't do things with them as part of the family.
When they went to the mall shopping, his son always walked
apart from the rest of them, as if he were ashamed
of being with them. Robert had tried to show him things
about an engine, how to maintain a car, but his son
was so inept with tools. Robert felt embarrassed for him,
always a little uneasy, there was just something different.

Philip was a good help out in the barn, though. His son
and his wife often did all the barn chores themselves,
milking the cows, pitching manure, bedding the animals
because he was at the paper mill. Summers, the whole family
worked together to put up hay. He'd taught his son
how to drive the tractor, run the mower and the baler.

Philip wasn't especially strong, but he did his part. He loved
to go fishing, any chance he'd get. That was masculine,
wasn't it?

But Philip had liked to do things around the house, too,
things Faith didn't have much time for or interest in doing.

Robert hadn't thought too much about it at the time. Faith and the girls helped out in the barn, so why shouldn't his son help out around the house? He'd dug up, planted flower beds, was always cooking. He loved to cook. Robert thought his son might grow up to be a chef in some fancy restaurant. Then there was that phase when he was sewing himself bow-ties.

Robert turned up the speed on the windshield wipers, trying to get rid of the streak left where they were worn. Should he have seen this perversion coming then? Should he have stepped in to be a more masculine influence? But Philip had had at least two girlfriends during high school, dates he'd taken to the high school prom, junior and senior years. He'd spent a lot of time in his senior year with that girl, Cindy, thought they might be serious, that she might be their daughter-in-law before long, but then Philip lost touch when he went to college. She was dating another guy now.

They were getting closer to town, starting to see billboards. "I should turn around, I should put an end to this," Robert thought. "I should take him back home and tell him he is not going to spend the weekend with his so-called friends in Duluth. He is not returning to that college in Iowa. I should not turn my son over to some stranger in the dark of night, who could do who knows what to him, who could have his way with him and then leave him dead someplace. I should take him home where he belongs."

But Philip didn't live at home anymore. He had moved out two months ago, after taking them out to the truck stop for dessert one night and announcing to them this thing

about himself so loudly that anyone in the restaurant
could have heard. He had told them he thought this
was God's way for his life. No, not God's way, The Good.
He believed in The Good. He didn't believe in God anymore,
at least not in their God. Faith kept telling him to keep
his voice down. Robert hadn't been able to say anything.

He certainly hadn't been able to eat his slice of pecan pie.
Philip had given them a four-page, handwritten letter
explaining his new-found philosophy. They couldn't
make any sense of it, other than that he was now
calling himself a humanist. And that he was a Sodomite.
They stayed up praying and searching the Scriptures all night.

The only thing they could decide to do was to tell him
he couldn't have his car on their insurance policy anymore,
that his newly chosen lifestyle made him a poor risk.

Philip's car was now in a garage in Duluth, getting tuned up
for his trip back to college. He'd taken a bus to visit them
to say good-bye, the first time he'd been back home since
he'd moved out. A guy he'd met in Duluth would meet him
half-way, in the parking lot of the mall in Cloquet, give him
a ride back up to Duluth. They were heading there now,
to meet this friend.

Robert wondered what this friend would look like. He realized
he had no visual image of these people. Had he ever met
anyone who was that way? He'd never thought about it.
In the army and at the mill, he'd heard guys talking dirty,
calling other guys faggots, but he never listened to that talk.

A chilling thought struck him. Could people tell by looking at his son that he was a pervert? Did it show?

"Raise up a child in the way of the Lord, and when he is grown he will not depart far from it." Robert repeated this verse over again to himself. "I cannot let myself believe that my son is a pervert. This is a rebellious phase he is going through," Robert told himself. "He's just doing this to push us away, to test us, to test God. We need to pray he will get through, grow out of this, and hope he won't get hurt."

They were at the driveway to the mall. Robert swallowed hard, turned into the parking lot. It was deserted, except for one other car, parked in the middle, under a light.

"That's Gary," Philip said.

"Gary," thought Robert. "Gary, my youngest brother, the one always getting into trouble with girls, into trouble period." He pulled over toward the car and parked a way away, his headlights on the driver's door. It opened, a male figure six feet tall emerged. "He looks like a Sunday School teacher!" Robert thought. "I am turning my son over to a man who could be planning to molest and kill him, and he looks like a Sunday School teacher!" The man was dressed casually, neatly. Light brown hair, medium length, his features soft, his eyes kind, sincere. He appeared to be about thirty. "The devil wears many disguises," Robert thought.

"Okay, thanks," Philip said, opening the door and getting out. Fear gripped Robert's stomach. What was he to do? Should he just sit here and let his son disappear?

He reached for the handle and opened his door.
He felt dizzy, disoriented as he got out, shut the door,
started walking toward the man. As he drew near
he felt a wild desire to punch the man in the stomach,
then on the jaw, to knock him down and start kicking him,
stomping on him. He wanted to yell at him, tell him to leave
his son alone while pummeling him with his fists.

Robert was a gentle man. He'd never been in a fistfight,
ever in his life, not even as a boy. He'd always walked away,
asking God to forgive him, to help him control his anger.
Robert's hand came out from his waist, toward the man.

"Hello," Robert said.

"This is Gary," said Philip. "Gary, this is my father."
Philip sounded excited, full of anticipation.

"Hello, Mr. Luing," said Gary, shaking his hand. "It's nice
to meet you."

Robert felt like the handshake was taking place ten feet away
from the rest of his body. He dropped Gary's hand, turned
to his son. He put his arms around Philip and clenched him
close to his chest, holding him for almost a full minute.

"We love you," he said, his voice raspy and guttural. Then
he turned and went back to the car. He got in, put it in gear,
pulled out of the lot. Around the corner, out of sight,
he pulled over, leaned his forehead on the steering wheel,
wept.

"That must have been hard for him," said Gary as he and Philip got into Gary's car.

"What?" asked Philip.

"Handing you over to me," said Gary.

"Oh, I just told him you're a friend," replied Philip, putting his hand on Gary's thigh and sliding over to sit next to him. "He doesn't know anything."

Chapter 3 — Dennis

Mt. St. Norma, Erupting

This would have been on my birthday in 1980. Dennis and I had just moved to Chicago from Portland, Oregon, and were still settling into our first-floor apartment behind The Bread Shop at the corner of Halsted and Roscoe. *Mt. St. Helens* had blown for the second time on the day that we drove east past it, just escaping the blanket of ash it was laying across the city of Portland behind us.

On the day of this story, we were bundled in blankets in the middle of a Chicago summer, lying on the bare wooden floor of the apartment because we'd not yet had a chance to go shopping for furniture.

Both of us had chills with high fevers from the flu, a bad flu. Dennis had been the first to contract it and was now alert enough to be able to hear, reach for, and answer the phone when it rang. The sound had barely registered with me in my far-distant place of sleep. I am a notoriously deep sleeper. As a child I slept through lightning striking the roof above our upstairs bedrooms. I'm told it was thunderously loud. The rest of the family, shaken awake and awestruck, gathered downstairs to decipher and reorient themselves to this powerful, dark-of-night event. When they realized in the head count that my nose was missing and unaccounted for, they panicked and ran up the stairs, only to find me sound asleep in my bed, unperturbed.

"It's for you," Dennis said, handing the receiver to me. Remember, this was 1980. More by reflex than aware of what I was doing, I put it to my ear and heard a weak, pinched, female voice on the far-distant end identifying herself as "Norma." The only Norma that came to my sleep-and-influenza-addled mind was *Norma,* the heroine of Bellini's opera by that name, sung gloriously by Dame Joan Sutherland.

My fevered logic told me the caller, then, had to be someone from the college from which I'd graduated the previous year, because it was there that I'd been introduced to *Norma* and the reverence due her. Only someone from my alma mater would know to call and employ that pseudonym to play a practical joke on my birthday. Except that I still couldn't identify the caller because I hadn't had any friends named Joan at college. I was still confused, and still none too cogent.

What ensued was several minutes of increasingly distraught beseeching, during which the caller adamantly insisted that she was neither Joan nor Norma, then just kept repeating, "It's Norma!" trying to get through to me. Finally, she said, "Here, you try to talk to him," and I heard a male voice begin to speak. I immediately recognized it as that of my father.

At that point I realized that the woman with whom I'd been speaking was indeed not a prankster from my alma mater, but rather my actual *mater*. "Norma" was, in fact, "Mama" who, despite fearing the worst, had gotten up her courage to call and wish me a happy birthday. I was struck by the humor of the situation and tried to explain the fractured logic of my fevered, deep sleep's associations to my father, then had what I thought was a decently sustained, fully coherent conversation with them both.

Unfortunately, despite my explanation, over the following weeks and months I heard separately from several of my siblings, each excoriating me for having been drugged out of my mind on my birthday. In fact, the only recreational drug I'd ever come close to experimenting with before, during, or since college was Iowan ditch-grown marijuana. Its aroma made my stomach feel queasy while its only effect was to put me to sleep. After a few tries, I decided that I much preferred using abstract expressionist art for my mental tripping. But I, their son, was gay and pantheistic, so I suppose that they, being of a fundamentalist, teetotaling Christian mindset, had to think that drugs were the only plausible explanation.

[illegible]

your sad eyes are the eyes of
the people on the street & I
loved them so and I thought
I loved you - but it was
the people in your eyes I
thought I could [illegible]

The Letter That Became Drawings

The three drawings emerged from my pen in the autumn of 1981, when I had sat down to write to Dennis after he ended our relationship as a couple.

We met in early 1979, during my senior year of college, and that autumn we relocated together from our home in Iowa City to begin our lives in Portland, Oregon. We leased an apartment above a shop named *The Foxy Lady* and both had secured jobs.

From the front windows of our apartment, we watched the transformation of *Mt. St. Helens* after its first eruption that winter. We first knew the mountain as a snow-capped, evenly symmetrical, inverted cone. Soon we began hearing reports on the evening news about increased seismic activity. Then a veil of clouds moved in, shrouding the peak from view for weeks. During that time, the volcano erupted, blanketing regions to the east of it, away from Portland, with volcanic grit and dust. When the clouds finally cleared, the mountain's shape had been entirely remade. The symmetrical peak was gone. In its place stood a jagged silhouette: dual peaks flanking a hollowed center.

Around this time, Dennis's employer offered him a promotion if he would relocate to the company's headquarters in Chicago. He accepted. Just six months after our westward drive to Oregon, we made the reverse trek east to Illinois. The very day we left Portland, Mt. St. Helens erupted again, this time spewing its debris westward and blanketing the city in ash.

In Chicago, through contacts at his new job, Dennis began to dip into the party-drug scene, though never in my presence, and without my direct knowledge. I went out to plays and poetry readings while he went out to parties. He was conflicted and soon addicted, caught between wanting more and wanting to protect me from his need.

I wanted to stay, to stand by him. He insisted that I move out on my own. That autumn, I assented. After we unloaded my belongings into my new studio apartment, I sat down to express my feelings to him in a letter, one which turned into drawings instead of words – two portraits and a four-page linear missive. Later, I would write a personal essay, ruminating on the first photo of himself that he had given me when we met. But I never wrote that letter.

A decade later, I wrote and delivered his eulogy when Dennis was buried in his hometown cemetery in Iowa. He'd stayed with Jeff and me after his first discharge from an AIDS ward, and I'd served as his caregiver until his death. After his death, his sisters in Iowa asked me to serve as his executor.

Photograph

For Dennis, 1981

Once again, I'm looking at the photograph he gave me early on—when I still needed one, before I no longer did, but now do again.

An odd photo: the only one he had that was at all current to our love. Two wizened old men—one in a wheelchair—sit quietly amid the clutter that is their life in this white-painted, oak-solid room of an aging Iowan house. Perhaps in another age these two would be sages or seers. The one with his crazed hair sweeping back and his wild whiskers joining, somehow, in anarchy to form a beard—he is more Tiresias reincarnate than any actor has ever conjured from a make-up box. In another age, perhaps. But here and now, they are lonely, and he has befriended them.

Hands in his pockets, he has placed himself against the doorframe, his posture something between standing and leaning. His clothes hang from his shoulders. His expression could be said to be blank, except that I have seen him wear it so often. His eyes belie his pretense of absence. They are directed slightly to the right of and beyond the camera, and I know that he is trying not to be beautiful.

Those eyes I will miss the most. Playing my fingers around his just-a-little-hairy chest, our warm, full lips inhaling each other's breath, the passion of our bodies pressing together driven by an always-unsated desire to press even closer. After the aching for those delights eventually dulls, as it must, still I will remember his eyes, because already they have endured longer.

He did not like for me to call him beautiful. He loved and feared his beauty, and probably never fully understood the beauty he possessed—the beauty for which I most loved him. The gentleness of his being was his beauty: his kindness, his hurt, his intelligence, his need, the soft touch of his hand. These were as much a part of his beauty as his ruddy pink complexion, sculpted features, and chocolate-brown hair—his iconic "Marlboro Man" masculinity.

He was incapable of cold beauty. When he tried to stand aloof—to be hard, cool, impassive, absent—it was the gentleness he tried to veil that ignited the beauty he radiated. He could be mean, selfish, a self-described bastard—at least externally—but whenever he was, his eyes spoke to a hurt he seemed to be trying not to know he felt.

I never saw him fully reconciled to his gentle nature, except perhaps sometimes, early on, when we were alone. He thought gentleness left him exposed, somehow dependent, weak. Perhaps that is why he couldn't be at ease with his beauty: to do so he would have had to admit and accept his gentle nature. Perhaps, too, that is why he had such sad eyes, so often full of hurt: he was always hurting himself a little bit, trying not to be what he so naturally was. He told me you had to be mean, you had to be a bastard to get ahead, and his eyes winced each time he said it.

He is getting ahead, he says. He would rather be writing. He wrote a short story once, which he shared with me. It was sensitive, impressionistic, honest, and totally revealing. I saw his eyes in his words as I read them.

I am not with him now, but his gentleness still is. Other people, good people, will see it and be drawn to him. I know that wherever he goes in his life, he will have the company of his own beautiful nature, and that I will miss him.

Amen.

Eulogy for Dennis Stephan Smith
Who died January 2, 1990

I am honored to share a few words of tribute to my friend of
over ten years, Dennis S. Smith, a man who loved words and
used them sparingly. I had the privilege of helping to put
Dennis's affairs in order, and I can attest to his devotion to the
written word. He saved any card, letter, pamphlet, any slip of
paper with words conveying some thought, idea, emotion, or
sentiment, even those criticizing him.

And then there were his books. My personal remembrance of
Dennis now includes a backache from carrying boxes and
boxes of them: the classics of literature, art books, stories of
the world's religions, histories ranging from American race
relations and the labor movement to accounts of ancient
Africa, China, and World War II. There were books on
economics, business, and self-study guides on everything
from real estate to gardening.

And, of course, there were the books on his preeminent
intellectual pursuit and passion: the Russian language,
literature, art, and history. Boxes of books in Russian, by
Russians, about Russia. How ironic that Dennis's untimely
death has cut him off just as *glasnost* and *perestroika* are
beginning to open us to that country which had so long
captured his imagination.

Dennis's life was full of ironies. That is how it often is for
people who pursue dreams and ideas. He collected unicorns,
and his life was filled with those idealized, elusive creatures of
the imagination. Life is not always easy for such dreamers. In

exchange for their visions, dreamers must sometimes forgo the sure footing that we, who lead more conventional and practical lives, so value. But our own lives would be much poorer without a few dreamers among us—to spark our imaginations, to stretch our understandings and leave behind a life we have to think about, write about, and stretch to understand.

In going through Dennis's papers, I came upon a notebook dated March of 1987 in which he speaks more eloquently than I can about how life was for him, how he viewed himself. In it, Dennis wrote:

> *He has the look of a dreamer, this Dennis Smith.*
> *His eyes have an "I wish I were somewhere else"*
> *look. His voice resonates confidently with an "I*
> *will soon be somewhere else" sound.*

> *This Dennis Smith is a man of ephemeral*
> *qualities: evasively loyal, lovingly evasive. A*
> *man imbued with contradictory qualities, all*
> *strong, but seemingly weak because of shifting*
> *emphasis on the many facets of his life.*

> *Love is the feeling that keeps me alive. It is the*
> *feeling I am fulfilled with, the feeling I am alone*
> *with, the feeling I long for, and the feeling I am*
> *short with. It causes me happy, sad, joyful, and*
> *painful nights and days. I am confident of it,*
> *confused with it. I need to have it but survive*

without. I would rather live than survive, though.

I care for my mother: of all the people in my world, she is the one I could always count on. I would do badly, and she would say, "I love you." I did well, and she said, "I knew you could!" I cried, laughed, and left. She said, "I love you."

I returned to her what I was capable of returning, when it was possible. She smiled and hugged me. As if she would live through me, my last promise to her was "to do something."

I can and will, Ma.

So, I write on! Write with! Write away!

To write is to commit. Put my thoughts on paper, and I'm committed. I look back on what I've written and am surprised at old commitments I have made and fulfilled, or not.

I commit when I write. As a person committed to growing and living, I write also of my changing opinions and of the growth that makes me human.

That provides a look into how Dennis saw his life. I cannot add much to it, except that I saw him die, and I can tell you that he died at peace. He nodded off to sleep for a nap, and as the hours passed he drifted further and further into his dreams. There were no shivers of fear, no cries of anguish. He simply and peacefully drifted beyond any need for us and our world.

In life he had needed his friends and family, though perhaps not in the conventional ways we might have wished to be needed. He pursued his dreams, he held onto every scrap of paper we sent him, and he died without apology, unafraid of death, at peace with himself and with his life.

It is now for us to live at peace with his memory, to allow his dreams to enrich our imaginations, to remember him and to honor him as the unique and special person we were privileged to know and to try to understand.

Farewell, Dennis. Thank you for sharing your dreams with us. May you rest in peace and in our memories.

Farewell.

Book 2

From Particles and Disputations:

Writings for Jeff —
A Book of Hours

Foreword

"Words, mere lines drawn on frail paper
(and this, they say, is how history endures?)"

When my partner Jeffrey died of AIDS on March 9, 1994, one
of my greatest comforts was sorting through and organizing a
drawer full of those "mere lines drawn on frail paper":
birthday cards, holiday greetings, anniversary remembrances,
various notes I had written, and a few he had written to me.

Jeffrey wasn't much of a writer. He had a gift for spontaneously saying what he was thinking, then showing by his actions what he meant by it.

I, on the other hand, have never had much of a talent for extemporaneous speech. I hold my tongue, hold onto my words, wait until it is quiet, then let them out bit by bit on little scraps of paper. Even then, I can't bring myself to let go of them until I've turned them over and over in so many ways that I delude myself into thinking they might finally say something close to what I mean.

We complemented each other well. He handled the phone; I took care of the written correspondence. And we learned to communicate with each other in many ways—often without either spoken or written words.

I hope this collection of writings I did for and about Jeff will now communicate to other readers, mostly by inference, the story of our lives together. I hope you will see how we grew as a couple, and how, through our struggles, we found or created spiritual meaning in our relationship. And I hope you will see something of your own relationships in ours. Especially in the early years, my words may strike you as effusive, idealistic, naive. If you roll your eyes, please do so with kind indulgence.

There are several people I must thank for making the compilation of this book possible. First, all those who stood by us during and after Jeff's illness and death. Their kindness and concern wrought much healing and reaffirmation of my spirit. I give special thanks to Jeff's family to his parents, his sisters, and their families who treated me and my relationship with Jeff with the utmost dignity and respect. They, along with our friends and the professionals and staff at Northwestern Memorial Hospital in Chicago, were truly partners with me in caregiving.

Finally, I must thank my present partner, Charles Stephen Hughes, for his immense generosity of spirit in encouraging me to work with these materials and for his sacrifice of time and attention I would otherwise have spent on him. And yes, I am now writing to and about him. Let us hope that when it comes time to collect those writings, they will tell the story of two men happily growing very old together.

[Written in 2002]

"...hidden in the tatters of my old, most favorite shirt..." (page 70) The photo is of Jeff seated on my lap in 1982 at our going away party in Chicago when we were about to move to Fort Worth, Texas for his training. In 1988 I fashioned the shirt I'd worn into a heart shaped Valentine which unbuttoned to reveal my writing, "Finding Love".

Chapter 1: *Matins — Young and Silly in Love*

May 1982

Dear Greatwhatwho'sityouare / God,

Did I ask for this, or is he a mistake? That is to say, he's short, almost an inch shy of my own modest height; not exactly the lover to whom I had assumed I'd look up. And though nuzzling his earlobes from behind as I peer over his chest and below does indeed provide unexpected delight, still:

There's the matter of his rather many muscles. Most noticeable. And most noticeably not restrained to abstracted realms of art or fantasy within the limits of which I had been safely wont to indulge in musculature unabashedly, whereas in actual flesh I had feared that muscle negated mind, rendering unknown risk. Absurd, of course, given him. Yet such perceptions abound, and I admit to certain qualms at my intellectual self being seen in intimate company with, ahem, a hunk.

So, though he makes a lovely model, as well as conversation most sincere, sensitive, and enlightening, his mind proving to be as solid as his muscle, still, somehow, I had just never imagined.

But then this thing we share, he and I, is how shall I say, well, so sweat-laden, so physical. Which is not to say it lacks spirit, but oh my God, he's such a crazy fuck! We do shoulder stands, headstands, handstands, climb up walls and find ourselves mounted midair as our tongues... All this I rather love, of course, but we've yet to discuss opera, the aesthetic orgasms to be had on hearing Sutherland sing Bellini's *Norma*.

And then have I yet mentioned his bald spot at age twenty-seven, with which I perplex myself by adoring? Or his crooked front tooth, which invests his flawlessly French face with intrigue? Or his childlike joy in life's simple pleasures, whereas I, myself, am personally most complex and tend to see shadows?

God, he grew up Catholic. How can I relate, having myself been reared by Baptists who taught me that Catholicism is a Communist plot? It's true we met in a less-than-orthodox church; still, I suspect him of Christian inclinations quite unlike my own pagan yearnings.

My God, there's me, the radical revolutionary pacifist humyn liberationist gay activist feminist philosopher poet, and he says he doesn't like labels, would rather relate to people as people. Which does make sense, in a way, I guess.

But he cuts fur. So, God, how can this man who deals in the dead carcasses of minks for the moneyed be appropriate for me, me who does not approve of a masculinist society's competitive structure for accruing wealth, who lives comfortably near poverty, and who thinks fondly of vegetarian ideals (though not quite yet to the point of practice)?

It's true, my own employ is at a gallery where many more can appreciate than can afford; and fur work, it turns out, is an ancient, intricate craft; and I must admit that nature's methods of population control are themselves cruel; and, looking down, I see I do wear leather shoes, which I hadn't considered.

But God, this I'd like to know: if this is love, just when did it happen? Two months becoming acquainted without even trying or noticing, and then this happens, and I can't even say when? It's disconcerting.

And if this is love, why isn't my life blown apart? My life was going along fine, I met him, and my life is still going fine. What is this? I thought love changed everything, like it or not. This just isn't at all what I had in mind.

All right, all right, so I prayed; you responded. Perhaps I wasn't specific. That will teach me to pray poetry: *"Come my lover with your gentle eyes,"* and *"let not my love dissipate on an always anonymous world but know the passions I possess though dare not always expose without a companion to love when the world seems not to comprehend."*

Okay, God, so I'll give you the eyes, gentle, joyous, wild, honest yet beguiling, sparkling with love, especially when they look on me. You did at least get the eyes right.

And his cuddles do ooze affection.

And our contours do coincide quite nicely as we sleep together, so soundly.

And really, if the truth be known, my God, I must confess that I find no fault in him at all, and that is more than just a little frightening.

But so be it, what it will be. Now I lay me down to sleep; I thank thee, Lord, this man I'll keep; and if I die before I wake, I'll go smiling.

Ah, a man, what a man amen.

DecemberSun #1 — *Enchantment*

(seasonal)

Enchanting this our first most-wonderment season together: we share the gift of us, now eight months since first unwrapped, now unwrapped again. We mark our first DecemberSun festival of the sun's cold birthing, blazing the logs of our desire to be a single flame undying, establishing by instinct what will be our personal ritual, observing through champagne bubbles the magic of sharing an ancient festival with newfound love.

Merry DecemberSun, my bold, enchanting love; may the observance of our passion see us through many a season of the sun's return.

A Toast to Orange Marmalade on Cherry Pie

Here's to the memories
 we've yet to make
 a moment or two of nooky
 we've yet to take.

Here's to Valentine's silliness
 we've yet to share
 (Like this verse
 it's gonna get worse.)

Here's to you,
 and me,
 and we whee, wheeee!!!
 (See?)

Here's to Christmas presents
 in July.
 Here's to orange marmalade
 on cherry pie.

Here's to arms that hold
 the world together
 when eyes cry.
 (Ah, that's nice.)

Here's to you,
 here's to me,
 here's to we, whee, wheeee!!!

Here's to play,
 here's to today
 and tomorrow 'wit chew'.

Cheers!

Anniversary #1 — *Bagels and Cream Cheese*

Remember Ricky's that night? Your friend, the waitress who, ten months later, we wished a good life with a twenty-dollar tip because we were leaving Chicago, brought us two buttered bagels with cream cheese and countless cups of coffee as we smoked our far too many same-brand cigarettes and exchanged conversation so intent on each other that not a single word on a single subject we discussed that night comes back to mind.

We were observed, I learned later from a close friend who was there though I didn't notice and he was more sensible than to intrude. But yes, our "ever so intense" connection was seen that particular evening in that then to become our sentimental favorite Jewish deli: that evening exactly one year ago today when the somewhat confused ex-Catholic in the church's study group became something more, my future now present lover, looking at a lifetime together.

So was it something you said, something I no longer recall that rendered the moments, if not the words, unforgettable? I have a vague recollection of something entrancing in your eyes that I hadn't seen before. All I remember distinctly are the bagels and, a few weeks later (still too soon), the impulsive first of innumerable I-love-you's offered to one another.

Also, I recall, after the bagels, our parting company in the midst of a Chicago drizzle. I don't recall whether the rain was warm or cold, but you boarded a southbound Broadway bus, and I walked north. We hadn't kissed, though we'd wanted to. Somehow the handshake knew it was and wouldn't be enough.

Now we make our love in our home in a place called Woodstock which we didn't expect to be in north Texas, but it is, and we do. There isn't much more I feel compelled to say on this occasion, except that our time together is now the happiest year of my life. I'll write more next year, and the next, and so on until, well, just until we have a very thick book.

Anniversary #1½ —
Silliness

Now eighteen months beyond the bagels of April 15 – has it been so little time that we are still celebrating it in months? Well, we must take care to be silly when we can, so happy eighteen months, looking on forever!

But how is it that eighteen months can contain all the times and places and stories we've been through together? Already our swaddling clothes are of a denser weave.

Our time together is still a preface to our vows, lest we forget. We've begun to discover how little we comprehend each other. Do you think you know me better than when we met? Are you content to call me mate? Do you know that I will change tomorrow, as I did yesterday, as you did, too? I love you more for all you've changed, but you are a mystery to me nonetheless. It seems the more closely we see things, the less sense they make, at least until our eyes focus on one another's.

This writing isn't done, but I think it's a good start. If I don't get a chance to write more before you get home, well perhaps leaving it at just a good start is more appropriate for the occasion anyway.

Happy eighteenth month, my love. Let's enjoy this silly occasion to its fullest and start to count the years tomorrow.

Chapter 2 — *Lauds:*
First Reflections

DecemberSun #2 — *Second Thoughts*

Merry DecemberSun, my love,
  as we uncork our second annual champagne morning,
  as we celebrate our second shared observation
  of the age-old winter festival of the sun,
  as our dreams of a future together begin
  to accumulate histories, realities, remembrances,
  perhaps even a surname: *Lafelaget* (lah-feh-lah-jay),
  roughly combining French and Old Norse
  to mean "the partnership and" – thus we are defining
  our love while keeping an open question.

To think that we can now look back
  over an intricate weave of days and events,
  months, seasons, places we've lived. The life on our loom
  already is rich with colors and textures,
  and our first DecemberSun observance is now but one
  of many sparkles in the emerging pattern.

Yes, Merry DecemberSun, my love, now here's a gift
  you can't unwrap: our history. And thank you, my love,
  it's a wonderful gift you've given me, this history.

It seems we've both managed to give the exactly, perfectly right gift to each other after all. How did we know?

Here's to our second DecemberSun, my love, and to our second very Happy New Year
– Cheers!

Perhaps

Perhaps the valentine I send you should be of highly polished wood, an object of calm, gentle strength, warm to the touch, full of life-enriched beauty because that would be very much like you.

Or perhaps I should send you the sky, across whose expanse an infinite and often incongruous variety of clouds drift, because that, too, would be like you, and sometimes you storm.

Perhaps my valentine for you should be a bright yellow daffodil, because that is how you like to see yourself, and how I like to see you too, especially on leisurely, sunlit mornings.

Or perhaps I should send you, hmm, cozy autumnal snuggles wrapped in flickering firelight, a big, shiny red apple for my favorite teacher, a meandering river of conversation for my closest friend, an endless moment of passionate embrace for my lover, a book of memories for our future.

Vows

Were we to exchange vows, what would we say? Perhaps it would have been better if we had spoken of love and respect when we were foolish, before we'd experienced their implications. Now our vows will demand more, and the words do less. Do you think we still have vows left to exchange, vows that can anticipate life, or will our vows have to wait; will we realize we've exchanged them only upon reflection?

Second Anniversary

Our second year: a year unsettled and unsettling, and our commitment is stronger for having seen it through. Remember, "If you felt that way, why did you hold my hand?" Now, looking back, the question answers itself. Yes, some storms we rose above; others we just waited out. "Jeffrey is dark today. He hasn't spat lightning, but..." Or, in your card to me: "Tears that are unspoken words... so sad and deep as you are." If we can penetrate the silences, we can usually get through the words.

It's been that kind of a year, you know? Mostly overcast. Sunlight on too few occasions. The Jephenfil Ficus tree dropped a lot of leaves, but its roots outgrew its first pot, and now there are a lot of new leaves coming on.

It was a year of getting out of bed too early on too many mornings. Not to complain, but it would have been nice to linger more often. Ah, but that speaks well of our desire, does it not? Had you not been at work on your birthday, the dozen yellow roses would have lost a bit of their place in our history.

Your parents came to visit, an important reconciliation for you and a successful first meeting for me. We traveled to New Orleans and went antiquing in Granbury. Our birthdays, DecemberSun, and Valentine's we marked most gaily, and we entertained with your tantalizing tetrazzini and my luscious leg of lamb. It wasn't all frustration, tension, exhaustion, and illness, though it was also a year for many hugs, for caring and taking care of each other.

Then are these the vows we're writing: to maintain, to get through it all, to put up with? Let's let there always be one more: to take pleasure in. Here's to our second year together, to the name we invented for ourselves, and to our third year coming on. Cheers!

Hide and Seek

You will not always find me in our hide and seek, not when I am the seeker and look for you in lonely corners only to discover other hidden things. I do not mean to lose you, but if I did not sometimes lose myself, how would I find anything? There's a vagabond's soul within this homebody with whom you've mated, a soul that does not always recall the most expeditious path home, and that is why sometimes I am lonely, even in your arms.

Chapter 3 — *Prime:*
Holding In, Holding Out

30th Birthday

I am writing this while sitting alone in a hotel room on the
evening of my first acquaintance with this place so special to
him, Appleton, Wisconsin, this small, green, clean city where
he was born and raised. It's fitting he should be here for this
thirtieth birthday, I tell myself. It's fitting he should be with
his family, his parents, sisters, and nieces. I, however, am not
fitting here. I am not at home in this situation.

Circumstances, i.e., the discomfiture of those related by blood,
dictate that I do not join him at the family get-together he's
attending. I can be visited, but I am not welcome to visit in
return because then I'd have to be explained. To his credit, he
accommodates such circumstances well, whereas I tend to
pout.

These words, these self-pitying words are not what I had
intended to write as his birthday message. His birthday
message, do you hear me? Why am I talking about you instead
of to you? Here in this place there is so much of you, and I am
an outsider, an onlooker, an observer. I am reminded that you
have known me for only one-fifteenth of your life, and I feel

inadequate to the occasion of your thirtieth birthday. This place asks me what I know of you, and it claims to know more.

Ah, but it's the arrival here that I share with you, for which I am proud of you, for which I love you, the arrival at thirty years as a man of compassion, persuasion, intelligence, sensitivity, motivation, memory, and promise, a man to whom I commit my love and future wholly, and our history together irrevocably. That is what I know of you, where I am secure with you, why I have mated with you, why I wish you a happy thirtieth birthday, and why I look forward to being alone with you and your reminiscence tomorrow, here in this place, your hometown, Appleton, Wisconsin,
with all my love.

Clarity

There are moments of intense, gentle clarity when everything is as it should be, when this life is the one I'd choose, have chosen. We make sense in such illumined times as all the chatter calms into a soothing hum. When I think of you, these are the moments I grasp and hold closely, hoping to believe that they are not all that extraordinary, only special, knowing the steps I take into them must be unstudied, unlearned, unknown, done: the necessary next of all that you and I and we are and want to be.

Dark Threads

There is, too, a dark, swirling space between us, many black threads entwined but as yet unknotted. And there is silence in the spaces between us, sometimes calm, sometimes turbulent. The crashing of ocean waves, always the crashing of ocean waves, that is the image that comes.

Knots

Knots tied in time do not easily unravel, my love, and we have tied into each other more than once. Fate has plucked from her mass of yarn the two we are to weave from them this cloth we call our story, and Fate's loom weaves many textures. This day's completion again promises tomorrow. I love when we wake in each other's arms, you know?

Context

If we yes us, then you are, I am; our context unfolds. Done doesn't reverse; any way we choose adds on.

Current Tense

No honest word is complete. How, then, can I tell you midstream how it is as the waters tug and pull?

Pricks

Does he excite me? It's an outrageous question. "Of course!" I scream. No, I don't scream; my mind screams. I sit passively, contemplating the syllables and the stained-glass shade overhanging the table. Something's breaking inside me. If I were to allow myself to get excited, I might be noticed. I might be disliked. Do I dislike excited people? Some, depending on how they handle it, how seriously they take their excitement. I don't trust myself to handle excitement well because I've embarrassed myself so often by taking it so seriously.

Creak, creak, ping. I am afraid of the flood, the gush, the explosion that's coming. Will it hurt? There's too much blood in my vessels and too much shit in my bowels; pricks are dangerous.

DecemberSun #3 —
In Truth, Not Fragile

Home here, our place secure, settled, and known. For that (as we again entertain these champagne memories) I love you, of course you know. Merry our third DecemberSun, my love; merry our third merry thee, me.

In truth: intricate, precious, not fragile, this love is a gutsy, robust, headstrong, die-hard creature, with a will to breathe. Open in the sense that it wills itself on beyond whenever and whatever we wish we knew but don't, can't, must "Plan A" and

"Plan B" to see what happens: wait, ready, open to possibility, chance, readying ourselves for our time to come.

Home here, our place secure, settled and waiting for us to come home together to reassure, recuperate, rest in one another, to hold together. We have our place here, we must care for each other here, we must continue as we have already done. Merry this our third DecemberSun, my love, what comes we are ready for, you know?

In truth, not fragile: the weave of daily, ordinary caretaking is thick. We give of ourselves to the home we build on our loom, a gift every day in the giving, the getting, the breathing. There is something here, a calm knowing for which I have no words to name: a sense not of beginning but of being in the midst of now, a continuity to which I am a most happy party.

Merry this our third DecemberSun, my love. I merry me with thee, with all my love.

Our Custom Becomes Us

Working its way from the inside out,
 that baffling sense of us
 to which we endeavor
 in good faith, with sturdy will,

to which, on celebratory occasions,
 we attempt to put words, mere
 flat lines drawn on frail paper

(And this, they say, is
how history endures?)

Mere flat lines drawn
from depths unfathomable,
with facets innumerable,
this churning, emotive, unworded story
of desire to mate, of passionate instinct,

erupting even now, spewing forth
as silly, scribbled hearts and flowers
on homemade valentines.

Melodrama

So, to what am I to attribute this abuse? Annoying little
people crawling all over us as soon as we sit down anywhere.
Bits of free-floating anxiety that one could swear look just like
people we know. We speak in bitter isolation and wonder
what he meant. Now he tells me I hurt him some time ago,
now, when it's safely beyond the examining touch. I am so
insensitive I did not know. Does he really believe his little
melodramas? I half do, so I suppose he's the same.

"Are you using me?" he asks.

"Come here, get in bed, and keep me warm," I reply. Ha. Ha.
I've had a beer and feel a little bold, plus we're both edgy after
our first full day without cigarettes. The words we'd inhaled
we now begin to speak, timidly but with vicious intent. Our
words are wicked, as are our silences. There are still so many

things to be worked out, and neither of us knows how to begin. What is it he expects of me, anyway, and why do I feel I must fulfill that expectation? Perhaps he wants to pretend that I'm not really crazy, or that I'm not a mistake and the cause of his sorrow.

Tangle

Events tangle; we two are thick as brambles. You've been around me so many times I feel an easy naked in your presence. Time's subtle tease is how the years possess us without notice.

Chapter 4 — *Terce:*
A Shift in Tense

Anniversary #3 — *Shoals*

My love, this is not a sentimental anniversary message, and in the days since I began working on it I have become less certain that it is appropriate to the occasion. More than I trust myself, however, I trust you, and I trust you will find reading these sometimes-painful lines to be a furtherance and finally a celebration of our mating.

Banished, I am standing drink-down, naked,
 legs spread, aiming
 for the thin strip of porcelain between
 the water and the rim, listening.

You squat, toked-up, naked,
 on the bedroom floor, a hand towel
 spread between your legs
 as you masturbate to magazine pictures.

I hear groans; I am pissing, pissed.
 We wonder what is coming of this.

What is required of this anniversary is reassessment, recommitment, renewal, the articulation of our realities, expectations, and finally our vows: vows of our passion to be ourselves within an entity which is us.

"I love you" is sometimes enough, but not to mask or excuse dissatisfaction. "I love you" is a transparent phrase. One sees through it to all the feelings for which we have no adequate words, and to all those for which we know the words but dare not speak them. Is not anger, too, a fundament of love? Were we not told this when starting out? Food kept too long spoils; opening the lid even a little lets you know. Perhaps we have sometimes been too patient with each other, held our tongues too long. We have known words of soured anger between us. I wish I understood more clearly what I am trying to say. I know neither of us has much taste for harsh words. They lump so in the stomach. But to say "I love you" with all its essential integrity – I do, you know, or I would not be writing this. For this anniversary, then, I give you my discontent and its corollary, hope for the future we are shaping.

I am discontented with myself. There are facets of me you must know, some of which make me wonder how you can love me, though I know you do. Apologies or promises to change would be inappropriate here; what we need first is simply to acknowledge the more difficult elements of our mating, then work from there. Here, then, are my confessions of internal turmoil:

I don't laugh and joke and act silly very often. My sense of humor tends toward the dark and the ironic. I am easily bored with tedious work, which leads to melancholy, frustration, low energy, light-headedness, and low initiative to change the situation. I forget important things that I need to do and procrastinate on unpleasant tasks. I'm a dreamer. I convince myself that things are how I wish they were. My head is frequently full of illogical imaginings and conversations, some of which I verbalize spontaneously. When I am alone, I shout incoherently, sometimes making vituperative remarks about myself, my parents, "America," people in general, and yes, even you, though I neither understand nor mean these outbursts. I have guilt/embarrassment attacks, inconsistent with or out of proportion to remembered events, and occasionally I will have periods when I run to a corner and beat on my head with my fists until I see stars. I am obsessive about reading, writing, and artwork such that once I've started, I can't get my mind to focus on anything else, not even you until I'm done or exhausted. My tastes tend toward moody, melancholy literature and art, the more abstract the better, and I criticize myself for being so morbid. I lack self-confidence, turn tension in on myself, and punish myself for feeling anxiety. Rarely can I lose myself in a conversation, and I especially do not communicate well on the telephone. And I occasionally yearn for a fuller exploration of my sexuality, but choose not to because of your insistence on monogamy, terms of our mating which I am willing to accept, but which can cause agitation, nonetheless.

Much of this you already know; some might surprise you. Can you still love me, anxieties and all? I know that you do, so perhaps the more practical question is: how can you more easily live with me? Perhaps by making these confessions to you I won't feel so compelled to protect you from myself in the future.

And so, as long as I am feeling brave, perhaps I should go the next step and stop protecting myself from you, too. Along with my discontent with myself, I have harbored complaints against you which I have been unwilling to share, but which we will need to ponder as we work out this mating. These are:

First, you do not always take well to correction, even of facts. I would like to teach you things, as you teach me things. If I act condescending to you, as you say I sometimes do, teach me a better way to teach you, and know that to belittle you isn't my intention or any way in keeping with my regard for you. I may feel more advanced than you on some subjects, as you are more advanced than me on others; that means we each have the capacity and responsibility to help each other improve ourselves individually and as a couple.

Also, you tend to dwell on your job, the difficulties, your qualifications, and how you're not being used to your full capacity. I know how good you are, my love, you don't have to convince me. You do sometimes have a tendency toward self-pity, especially when tired and under chemical influences. You are not always honest with yourself or me regarding this, making resolutions we both know won't be followed through. Optimism, which is something I love about you, carried too far can venture into untruth and lead to disappointment.

Finally, sometimes you are impatient with me when I don't live up to your standards. Usually you don't say anything, unless I pry, but you become cool and distant. Then I know I have sinned, but don't always know how.

Enough, enough. We are by far more joy and promise than what my confessions and complaints may seem. These are troublesome lists, perhaps inaccurate or exaggerated; it doesn't completely matter. What matters most is that we chart these waters, navigate these shoals. Every river has its rocky areas where its waters spread thin. Time and steady resolve will displace some of these stones and wear rough edges off others. All I ask is that we respect the danger of this river even as we experience its exhilaration. Are you with me, need I ask?

"In truth not fragile..." Happy anniversary, my love. I am very pleased to be here with you now, and I look forward to being with you for a long time to come. May these few dark lines of discontent be set in a book thick with joy as our love and mating endure. What say you, yes?

Judgment passed

The place looks good, our chores completed, almost. Then to sit and watch you burn the thing, to watch your eyes glass, and to see your smile break wide out in impish, faraway delight. That is the judgment you pass on me for my having failed to unwind, even with you, for having failed to laugh out loud and beg for your profane, perversely hare-lipped "merthy!" – for having failed delight so often. Now I think I know what you've been through, and I think I'd let the joint go to hell just for another fun evening with you.

Standing by

Again, he reports pain, and good-bye. I am left concerned and helpless, questioning the source. Am I the virus or merely the bereaved? No bystander, I stand by, I participate, I listen to each report, and I hurt. I can tell you about this pain he feels, and I cannot reach it.

Reflections

Scattered reflections of you and me flicker across waters troubled daily by fish.

Withdrawal

Silence, not animosity, fills the distance between us. I hope that what is, is not, or will not be if I don't mention it. If fears can be kept unspoken, we can confuse ourselves with vagueness, excuse ourselves from addressing our demons. What's coming into focus, despite my diffusing efforts, is a picture I'd rather not see, explanations for why things are this way that fit uncomfortably well. I feel threatened, foolish, monstrous. I want someone to read my poetry, to wrestle out of me my shy intellect, to tease me away from my self-consciousness and teach me to play.

Jeffrey, I would this would be you, but I'm not sure it can be. Where we're different, we're different; where similar, we're weak, and silent most everywhere these days. I feel like an injurious habit you're afraid to break. Perhaps this venting

will be enough to forestall a crisis. I wonder if we can loosen
our grips on each other enough to hold together, and if that's
what we want. I have a deep fondness for you (this, the classic
symptom of withdrawal?). Is it love? Sufficient and
appropriate to sustain the bond we profess? To weather my
boredom? I feel selfish and petty if I complain about the
anxiety, boredom, and loneliness I feel, and I rebuke myself
for dwelling on ill thoughts, for being obsessive about my
uncertainty and unhappiness. I tell myself not to think about
it, but of course, I do. (How many times have I covered this
same ground in my journals?) The question, Jeffrey, is: am I
what's wrong with us, or are we part of what's wrong with me?
Why do I ask you to be my hero? Can I not be my own?

Thirty-one

Time gone left empowered,
 your face handsomely lined (but lightly,
 lest you think too soon for this,
 your birthday at thirty-one).

At thirty-one, still lean, your body's
 polished-wood's smooth warmth,
 how firm my hands would ever more often
 hold your body close next to mine.

To be as we are when we are one sensory unit,
 each within our own private passions,
 joined within our male-mated pleasures.
 I am so proud of you, you must know how

I thrill to think the man you are, my mate,
inside this life, inside this life, inside
a common enough mystery, we share a certain love,
often unspoken, on occasion outspoken.

Inside this life we share a love settled
beneath the surface whys and wherefores.
This is the love I'd choose again.

Resolution

Today's completion becomes tomorrow, a fixed object shifting
in and out of focus.
Eyes weary, eyes brighten, emotions blur the picture. A steady
grip. We have the facts, we know what we are about, mostly,
enough. There is a sense of doing our best at the moment.
Tomorrow comes soon enough, next year is not tomorrow,
and we ready ourselves for both.

Significance need not thunder its occurrence. He walked out
of the meeting as a new man, wondering what to have for
lunch and when to wash the bathroom walls. I heard the news
and thought, "Well, that's that, at last. What shall we have for
dinner, and when will I do the floor?"

Analysis

Reaching back, I find that I am a more interesting history
than I had imagined. I am a creature of murky depths, still
surfaces, of contained torment. Alone, I erupt; in the presence

of others or another, I maintain calm, lose my anguish in taking care of others. This makes me difficult, perhaps dangerous, to be around; I project my pain onto others so I can nurse it, give to others the comforting that I crave. I wonder if there is a single, primary source of the pain, or if it is the accumulation of minor scratches left untreated.

Jeffrey, too, harbors great reservoirs of pain, which he used to turn through some innate alchemy into delight with life. Have I made him forget the formula? How do we rediscover the key to turning pain into joy? Is it so simple a combination as love and trust? We both keep secrets from each other, things we know, think, or do, things of which we are not ashamed but fear the other won't approve; things sexual, emotional, intellectual; things in our past and in our present. Perhaps we'd be more secure in our privacy, our private sense of ourselves, if we were less afraid of letting each other into our secret worlds.

Rings

Ring upon annual mysterious ring, recording the mystery of time's passing. The more I go on with you, the further back into you I get.

DecemberSun #4 —
To Be Continued

My love, our love is a merriment to be continued with each
DecemberSun we see ourselves grow; now four times have we
seen the sun come back together, and I believe in us as I see
the sun. This yes, too, to be continued. This is the season of
renewal: our DecemberSun song is silent music we hear when
we touch, a joyous sound like the speaking of each other's
name in our sleep. This is the season of renewal; we celebrate
our every new yes under the every new sun. Merry
DecemberSun, my love, with all my love.

Brooding

Brooding over needs held close, I (or who else might) dare
little speak for fear he (specifically or in my mind
conceptually) might not. We overdrink regularly, as it is, and
in nothing talk until the dullness weighs into sleep's respite of
unknowing until the always-again morning's thickness
demands endurance of the next day's light hours until the
next evening's first drink. Of course this must change, we
know. Stagnation is decay; it does not stay still but declines
inexorably and by tedious increment. We are falling down and
apart together, he and I, have been for some time. Or, if we
choose, our vows of renewal are not impossible, but thin if
spoken alone and repeated too often. What is this life we've
made for and of ourselves if it should so easily dissolve in an
alcohol solution? Nothing happens alone, but always in
conjunction. Instead, we need to urge toward light and joy,

mere pleasure in the being of ourselves. Into the larger picture
might we meander happily, our significance minimal enough
that we might enjoy ourselves and our being together. Amen.

Special Delivery

My love place inside my lips
your elegant, lean parcel; unload
in this male this morning I see
my valentine comes full heavy, and sweet.

Now to you, how shall I post mine?
If I cream-scribble silly love swirls
in your coffee, will you read my love,
or hear love whispers at your backside
as from behind the blinds I watch
you weather your way each morning,
always to work first?

This I know you know, my love:
we do our daily doings not unaware
that this life-is-love is more
than the sex we chance and plan to share.

But I admit your maleness so easily
excites my own to tell its lusty truth,
that when we're so entirely naked
in mind and body, I adore you most.

Anniversary #4 — *Prelude*

My love, in this past year we lost two cats, gained a worrisome virus, drank too much, continued to smoke, overworked and overstressed ourselves in pursuit of our careers, and let our sex life down too often. How does the St. Francis Prayer go?

Anniversary #4 —
Uneasily Unspoken

Having gone fourth into what is too often an uneasily unspoken love, we see that love is a daily decision we make, each on our own, in conjunction with the other. Today will I love best or hate most that whose loss I fear? We've no choice but to decide each day how we will engage the apparatus of our life together, with what machinations and with what intentions we will submit to influence the quality of our day. Time passes such that it is never lost; what's done is done and remains with us, not accusing, not congratulating, waiting for however we decide our present tense.

We must, we do make our decision, my love; we do engage ourselves in today's unfolding. So let's be real for each other, let's engage our issues and own our decisions. That which we hold together we cannot hold against each other. We own our mistakes as we own our successes, and we've brought far more of both together than our mere four years would tell. It is said that joy, unshared, diminishes; the opposite is true of sorrow. Certainly we've known both and have shared many. Do you trust me? Do I trust you? Then, only then, let's speak more of our silenced emotions, shall we? Joy is the other side of sorrow; we cannot bury one without burying the other.

Oh, we are a complicated lot, you and I both. I love you and know love is no one thing but many and varied functions of the survival instinct. Well, then, shall we survive and thrive together? Happy fourth anniversary, my love, and may we see tenfold and more, at least. With all my love.

Anniversary #4 —
Postscript

Our intimate, mere four years together, said in a promise, is to be ourselves and know precisely that is what we desire most for ourselves, for each other.

Path

Soothe the strains, relax; enjoy walking the trail green, moist, cool, nervous, wanting too much to be content.

Shared Vision

To see from inside the object of our vision is to meld, to inhabit the space we see around us: little purposes, little solutions, assertions and essays within a context overlapping our own. I write this as an attempt to resolve the astigmatism of our shared vision, to conquer my sense of inadequacy which imparts an occult quiver in whatever we foresee for ourselves. What alienates me from a sense of purpose is my fragile, grandiose imagination. I'd rather a truth be suspect than simple.

Success

Jeffrey, my love, in knowing you I have known success. I have held your goodness in my arms and felt its steady pulse. The mystery of you is how, with such unassuming ease, you are a quality so many philosophers have strained to decipher or define, and I am so fortunate as to observe every day being: you are good, and your success is in your goodness.

Every day we learn, we change, we grow, and on special occasions we reflect on how special our ordinary experience is. On this special occasion, your thirty-first birthday, I want to say how fortunate I feel to be with you and to wish you a happy birthday, my good, good love, with all my love.

Elements

To hear what is, touch context; sense the particular to which we relate, these particular sensations which constitute our life. Our strength is in our holding, our ability to hold together the elements of our love: concern, patience, boredom, charity, security, safety, frustration, passion, fantasy, self-denial, comfort, exhaustion, yearning, protection, loneliness, hope, optimism, disappointment, definition, humor, daring, communication, excitement, mutuality, exploration. Touch,

and we embrace wholly our history in moments pressed,
pressed in tangletongue lips, we kiss.

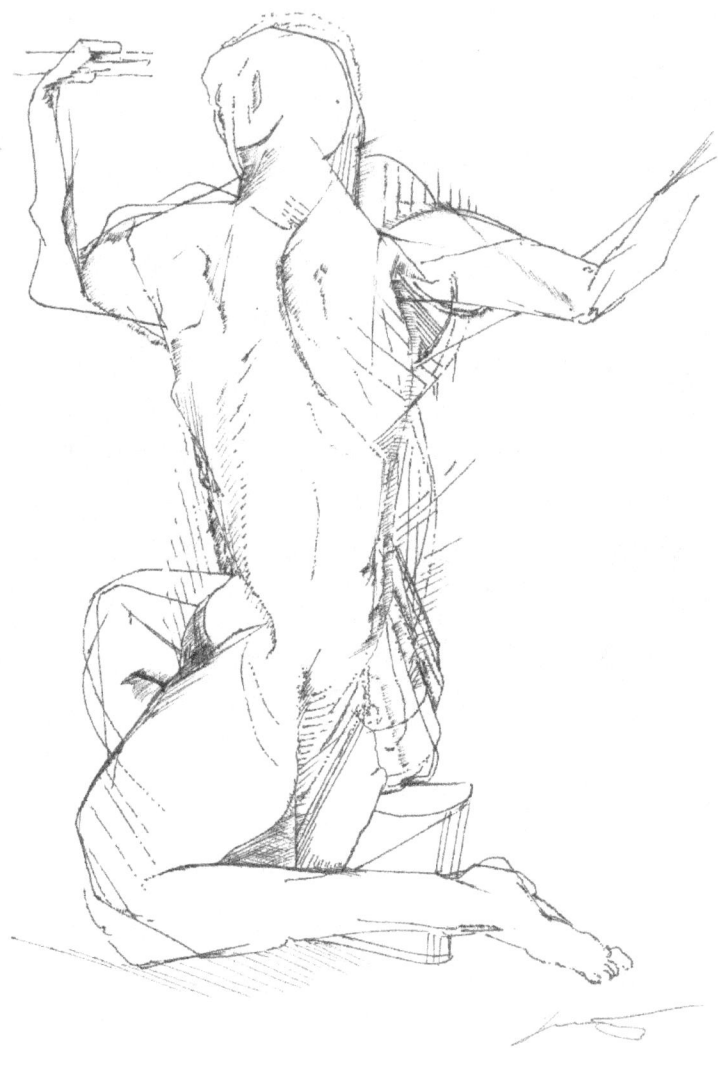

A sketch I drew from Jeff doing his daily calisthenics

Chapter 5 — *Sext:*
At the Apex of Life

DecemberSun #5 — *Nesting*

Merry our fifth DecemberSun, my love, merry amid our gifts
we unwrap particles, strands, laughters and disputations. Our
histories are remembrances into that which we are in which
we hatch our hopes and drop our droppings. I am yours to
unwrap, my love, I hope you find that which gives you joy,
might make you laugh, might take flight with your most
playful spirit, might ever renew your delight in our mating.

Nidification is our present business here this season, and the
next, and again the next. We must unwrap each other, my
love, and wrap our unwrappings to make our nest. We must
take care to gather that most pertinent, to wrap the strands
together, with friction enough to hold open enough to breathe
through many winds, so the weight will support itself,
ourselves, through another season and many another new
year of merry unwrappings.

Merry DecemberSun, my love; may we merry in our new year
of nesting, I with you, and you with all my love.

Roots and Blossoms

My love returns this Valentine's Day
  to changes we've set ourselves about:
  to refresh in mind and body, home and memory;
  to recall the promise of a gay daffodil
  in bouquet with a thorny, purple-red rose.

My love and I, through every change, have grown
  more intimate of root and history,
  yet to tell why he blooms bright, bold, open
  while I blush deep in a slow unfold,
  or how two men of such different blossom
  could share happy root in our common ground
  cannot be told, but given tender cultivation
  sometimes digging in, sometimes digging up,
  weathering weather foul and fair, we do.

I welcome your return this Valentine's Day,
  my love ever changes inside me, inside you
  stirs anew life's desire to be each our own
  full flower at intimate, deep-rooted ease,
  a bright daffodil and a murky rose joined
  this Valentine's Day in our ever-so-gay bouquet.

Anniversary #5 — *Reassertion*

Today we are five years intimate. What words can review,
forecast the complexities of two lives five years joined? Here
we are now in the midst of major change, a realignment of our

lives. We have grown circumspect and have opted to assert responsibility for our future, you for your physical health, and I for my self-respect.

So when, during these past five years, have we not been in the midst of major change? What day has passed that did not significantly increase our history together and invest in our shared future? We are always making ourselves: making breakfast, making love, making conversation, making our home, making plans, making sense of what we've done and are becoming. What did we know of where this mating would take us when we became intimate over bagels five years ago today? What do we know today of where we'll be five years from now, of what chords and scales in what octaves time's fingers will have played on the keyboards of our emotions? All I know is that so intricate and wide-ranging an overture promises a masterful symphony to follow.

Exhilaration, despair, abandon, alienation, trepidation, the blossoming of dreams, the rumblings of rude reality, the quiet contemplation of a point-and-counterpoint duet – all these we've known. We've marched in syncopated steps, each to the beat of our own different drummer, and we've swept across the floor in a fluid, singular-motion waltz. Throughout this piece, somewhere in the orchestration, we've maintained the insistent, erotic tension of our male on male tango.

My love, I'd meant to be more specific, to have named the people, places, and events of which our five years together are composed, to have named the many facets of you I have had the joy to discover and have the future to explore, to have detailed the depths of my love for you and my appreciation of our being together. I had meant to be more specific, but when in these past five years have you known me to be specific? I love you, I'm glad to be with you, and I hope to be with you for a very, very long time. That's about as specific as I can get. The rest is an ever-present, constant whirl of memories and dreams, possibilities and anticipations: a mad, beautiful confusion at the core of which pulses the mystery of our coupling.

Happy anniversary, my love. The Fates are playing our song, our wild, passionate symphony. Let's listen for the many, many more years to come. With all my love.

33 Wishes

May your sense of humor sparkle; may your goodwill toward people keep strong; may the current of your self-confidence carry you through each day; and may you find peace of mind in your recollections, and in your expectations. For this, your thirty-third birthday, I make thirty-three wishes, each being for your peace of mind; may they come to truth, and may I, too, find my way there to meet you.

DecemberSun #6 —
Sweet My Love Rest

Sweet my love rest, this holiday day comes a soothing relief, pause—the weary across our brows comes peace, peace. Glitter our champagne gifts, in open exchange our love, memories, regrets, and expectations are cuddled and dismissed, laid to rest amid festive wrap the cat plays with amusements of the very gay season most vulnerable, our underbellies exposed wide open, we assume the sweet, gentle rub, loving tickle; our pleasures prevail on each other's indulgence.

Come, sweet my love relax into this holiday day bathes us with essential goodwill, each one for the other – that you will have the best life possible for you to have, and that that life will continue intimately connected to my own, that is my best holiday wish for you, with all my love.

Finding Love

My love, may you find my love, even if this Valentine's Day you find me hidden in the tatters of my old, most-favorite shirt, serious behind one of my serious faces, or in a shadow, afraid to call out but hoping you'll find me to persuade me to play Valentine's Day folly in earnest in the bright, melting warm sun. And when you find me, my love, may you also find in yourself is the love I care for most. Even when you can't see my eyes through their curtains, I can tell you sometimes how much I all of the time care for you, and how glad I am to have found your love: how firm, steady, firm around my love it holds; how firm, steady, firm it holds my love.

Sixth Anniversary

Your name is now six years thick with meanings complex to my ears soothing, your name evokes the mystery of what we are to be to each other: friend, confidant, tease, scold, consort, educator, companion, friend. With you in my arms in your arms I feel secure, comfort, hope for our future; hope that I am for you, too, a safe harbor, your coming home a happy man.

That this may continue to be, my love, may we progress with comprehension, encouragement, to each other's ears may our names always be a fascination, words cherished, intimate, luxurious in the mystery of their significance, words, the meanings of which only we know, and each day must relearn.

34th Birthday

I love whatever makes you you makes you glad to have lived already longer than did Jesus Christ, for example—and without regrets, because you laugh, because laughter makes you ever more sure of yourself, of the pleasure and pride to be taken in how you've lived your thirty-four years, blossoming in each moment of your life.

Happy birthday, my love. May each day's circumstances compel your good humor to the fore, and may I continue to share with you your life, with all my love.

DecemberSun #7 — *Reprise*

More solid on this, our seventh DecemberSun festival reprise memories ever more substantial, intricate, and complicated in meaning. We celebrate, steady, mourn, encourage, and absorb again the years that were and those that will be: what we would and would not have come to be, but together will and together will through. I ever more solidly know more comfort in the intangible, physical fact of us.

Celebrate, my love; our meaning we each day hold close in each other's arms we feel support, even when apart we celebrate our love in the everyday doing, aware that on special occasions we will attempt special words for ordinary events, will glitter light through champagne-fluted perspective on this particular, our seventh DecemberSun together – Cheers!

Lonesome Valentine

Today, my love, you're off to your Big Apple business affairs, leaving me and the cat alone to remark to each other on this, our lonesome Valentine's Day. Love reveals the distance between us, defines it, invests terrible mystery in the fact of it. If we did not care so deeply for each other, we would not notice the spaces that separate us—spaces that ordinarily separate people in ordinary, casual relationships. It is our very longing to be one and special with each other that makes poignant and apparent the ultimate impossibility of realizing absolutely that desire. We long ago discovered that one and one make three, not one; there will always be you, me, and us at work in our mating.

Today is a day for us, but you are with you, I am with me, the cat is the cat, and we are all feeling lonely. So we cherish this loneliness because this physical distance reminds us of how important and affirming is our desire to communicate across it, to signal our recognition of each other even when we are unable to see each other distinctly, to traverse, bridge, or merely chart the distance between us, to throw a silly, cut-out paper heart from here to New York and back and watch the distance diminish, if not disappear. Happy Valentine's Day, my love—I await your return, with all my love.

Anniversary #7 —
A Deepening Blush

For Jeffrey, my love, who seven years ago blushed vulnerable across the room and years since Lucy's words still echo, suggesting what weights you must lift at the gym to manicure your handsome physique. But no, you counter, embarrassed, mere push-ups and sit-ups in your own living-room, calisthenics – real strength, your blush protests, with muscles toned years deep. Yours is not a superficial, designer-labeled body, it is your character, now suddenly made visible to me.

This seventh anniversary I celebrate that moment, the deep red blush whose power still carries me across these seven years in your arms, suspended in the clarity of the moment when I first recognized your essential reality, the solid, honest strength of your character.

In this moment seven years ago, I do not yet know that we will love each other, do not recognize sexual desire for your body, am not conscious of my own being. As an eye first looking through a microscope, I exist as pure wonder and amazement. I cannot take my eye away. Amazement is all that is real. I am thrilled at the moment of a great discovery and know that I must and will know more, and soon. In this moment, I do not know that we will go for bagels and cream cheese after rehearsal this evening.

For seven years now, my love, we have known more, have realized love and physical desire, have discovered many simple truths and complex realities about each other, ourselves, and our lives together, and have made of each discovery-moment our history and our future. For all the particulars and specifics of your life that I now know, you remain a wonder and a fascination. Each ordinary day, each passing week and season, each anniversary we mark special, I follow as your face, body, words, silences, energies and atmosphere swirl and stir, storm and calm, eddy and breeze across the peaks and ravines of my own topography. For seven years now, my love, we have weathered each other and remained as constant as the weather – always there, always changing, on occasion inaccurately predicted.

Yes, my love, whatever we are to each other at any given moment, we are constant, we maintain. We have seen seven years of change during a stage in our lives when change happens big – but are we seven years different from the two who sat at that table at Ricky's, oblivious to the rest of the world?

You are to me the same man whose blush compelled my attention, whose accomplished physique spoke of integrity, the formidable, calm, gentle, compassionate, honest, and resilient strength of your character. You are still the man I loved at first blush.

Happy anniversary, my love, may we continue to discover in each other that which compels our love to maintain and to grow. With all my love.

Thirty-fifth Birthday — *An Honest Word*

How can I connect with the thirty-five years of your life except through an honest word? What we hold between us becomes truth, our reality, our significance. What we say to each other we are to each other, and to ourselves. My connection to the thirty-five years of your life compounds with each word we exchange, and with each silence, because at this point silences have become words, too. To celebrate a life so close to my own, I must choose honest words and choose them carefully.

But words are fluid, animate: they shift in the light, carry shades and shadows of meaning, and relate to reality the way we relate to each other. Sometimes one must not be too careful with words; one must let them out to find their own ways home, like the first time we let loose the naked "I love you" – not considering where it might go or how far and for how long we'd be following those seven escaped syllables: *I love you. I love you, too.*

So here I come to celebrate your thirty-five years with words that escape me: joy, delight, pleasure, excitement, security, honesty, truth, trust, belief in each other, hope. As I write, these words shift context, cast shadows and implications, remind us of times when, absent or at a distance, they urged us to be ever more vigilant and yet more careless in order to discover their meaning, to lean toward the light thrown back on our faces as we follow them over our horizons.

My love, I am proud to celebrate your arrival at thirty-five as a man of humane accomplishment, steadfast loyalty, innate goodwill, and exemplary stature in both physique and spirit. Happy arrival, my love. May I share your arrival at many, many more, and at each celebration may I give you honest words to mark the occasion, and together throughout the years may we discover their meanings for ourselves.

Happy thirty-fifth birthday with all my love.

Intercourse

I am words you speak into me your warm breath wraps your
arms are words around me, your penetration sears through
my pain to understand inside my mind you come home to me
with words unguarded, and again I come home to you, and
again I am unguarded words you speak all around me to know
me more intimate of being as we drop our words into the
stillness around us, sweating this knowing how we have mixed
cerebral fluids to sweat our words over each other, and again
you come to me with your words, which I receive like love.

Chapter 6: *None —* *First Shadows*

DecemberSun #8 – *Split Vision*

Rings around this DecemberSun, my love, dark rings and light split our vision, bring us around again to another season again to where we start over again to where we carry on our celebrations a little askew, off-kilter, reeling rings around this DecemberSun season when sometimes not only the sun is diminished, and other candles need be lit.

Dark rings around our eyes this DecemberSun, my love, we weary in the chase to the festival's eve, weary to when we will collapse into each other's arms to hold together our being together through this marking of this ancient festival when the ancients' sun required them to light blazes in the longest night lest they not see the new, welcome dawn.

So, too, we light our own blazes, my love, make bonfires of our doubts, fears, exhaustions, and losses – blaze delight defiant against whatever dark rings us in the night, assert the light of this DecemberSun festival to soothe ourselves through to our own most welcome, well-rested dawn, when I would you could awaken with the sun refreshed, with all my love.

Source

Inside our so often and again arms
  wrapped intimate around each other we hold
  with unknown safety a fierce, maddening desire
  to tame this familiar stranger, this source
  draws our lips to vacuum-seal the taste
  of each other's saliva within our own, urged
  by innate need we seek to sate this desire
  to hold, to mate, to trust another inside us
  so often and again, wrapped intimate around
  inside our unknown selves.

Anniversary #8 – Spontaneous Harmony

I wonder at these rings we wear on our fingers now, how it
came to be that by our eighth anniversary we should have
matching rings, eight being a number for which I think
neither of us has any special regard. And we didn't get the
rings for our eighth anniversary; it just happens this eighth is
the anniversary following the acquisition of the second ring.

I suppose we could have more precisely marked the
significance of exchanging these symbols of our union –
thrown a party, sent announcements, concocted ceremony,
but I rather like the way they happened, more out of need
than convention. The set came into being not unlike our own
mating: we notice, we're aware of a void that needs filling,
begin searching, take tentative steps, add, amend, discard,

start over, act on an impulse that seems to have something special about it, it's working but needs something more, yes, still good, keep going with it, yes, it's right, complete enough for now. We'll let it rest a while, add on to it later, perhaps.

That's how the artist froze the craggy flow of molten silver to become the ring you purchased for yourself, which I acquired from your jewelry box, which after several rejections of other rings it occurred to us we should have copied but in gold for you, then again you had copied in gold for me. And so it happens that we now have a matched set of one-of-a-kind rings, to which we may someday add diamonds, or not.

These rings have become our story, their design the unpredictable, spontaneous harmony of a liquid flowing around obstacles, holding thick in places, spreading thin in others, yielding forms shaped by the innate tendencies of the materials within circumstances set by a creative free spirit. These rings not only celebrate our union, they also embody it.

And, in fact, we did celebrate their acquisition, as I recall. You have always looked good wearing gold and nothing else, but the first time we wore only these rings while making love, you were more beautiful than I'd ever seen you. Looking from your hand to mine and back to yours, not only our fingers entwined. Happy anniversary, my love, may we wear these rings and our love through many another.

Thirty-six

Thirty-six years into your life's adventure
 opens a year not to put off, to keep ambitions untold,
 a year for you to speak your hopes aloud, admit
 the fullness of your passions, a year to live
 your story completely, with each word more compelling.
 This is my birthday wish for you at thirty-six,
 a wish I hope to share with you throughout this year
 and through many another to follow, with all my love.

DecemberSun #9 –
Amid Shorter, Darker, Longer Days

My love, this DecemberSun season we circle like the free-form
flutter of ornamental doves atop our holiday tree. In uncertain
orbits we fly through this to-be-festive season amid a
coincidence of lights in profusion sufficient to assert, if not a
sealed promise, then at least, hope still visible.

What we need, we hold to each season provides new fuel to
maintain those first fires still burning as sparks rekindle
others. We light lights reminding us of our shared condition,
this need to care for each other, to hold watch through each
shorter, darker, what seems longer day, to comfort and
reassure through each urgent, fevered, sweat-soaked night,
and to celebrate with ornament and ornamental record
 this season of wonder and renewal, now the ninth we have
observed together.

Merry DecemberSun, my love, with all my love.

Question

My elegant valentine, if not for memories of having rounded
my palms down the curves of your physique, and if not for the
clothes you still look as good to me wearing as taking off; if
not for remains my desire to have your aftersex essence seep
over my skin, lingering like mind-wanderings rolling around
naked-smooth in silk my elegant valentine, would you still be
mine?

Well, would you?

Sometimes now, when sex is not possible for us anymore, I
wonder at how our love remains so potent. But it does. Yours
is still the only body at whose every touch I feel delight, and in
whose embrace I feel whole.

Happy Valentine's Day, my love with all my love.

Ninth Anniversary – *Travels*

My traveling man down nine twisty, fast, long little years all
over the somehow road we keep moving along, my traveling
companion whom I'd still like to take on a journey all over my
body through every layer of skin, do you realize how many
layers of skin we must have rubbed off each other over these
nine years of rubbing ourselves down this road?

I wonder how I might travel inside your mind, get my way
down some alley that's never been open for business before,
find my way up to somewhere inside you I didn't know I'd

want to be but am glad I managed to find anyway. Would you still come home to me if I got there, I wonder?

The thing is, there's always you, and that's always home, even if I just get up to go for a walk, step out for a bit of fresh air. Somehow it's become our own fact that we can never leave home entirely anymore, and never at all without a kiss.

Hold on, hold on—your hold on me holds strong, like a soft look, my love, my man who takes me to an easy sleep, fellow traveler to a free thinker, philosopher's companion, intimate friend, comfort. I would translate you into any language that someone could comprehend to tell how it is that I figure into your story, too – but some of that I may make up on my own.

I'd like to tell you what we'll find over there, how long we'll stay, what happens next, but some things a body can't know until you go and find out for yourself, you know? It's time for us to travel, my love, to wander inside each other's interior avenues and beyond our horizons, time to make friends with the road inside and out.

I can't tell you what we'll find out there, but whatever we find, I know we'll always find ourselves together at home.

Happy ninth anniversary, my love. May our journey take us through many another, with all my love.

Thirty-seventh Birthday –
An Apology

On this, your thirty-seventh birthday, before offering you my birthday wishes, I must offer you an apology for almost having lost myself and our celebration in one of my melancholy moods. What I would most like to give you for your birthday is an enduring enthusiasm in myself for my own life, similar to the joy I've always taken in yours.

Our birthdays come so close to each other by date, so far apart in our approach to them. Can you forgive, survive my somber brooding, protect the optimism in which your happiness finds root even when I thoughtlessly pluck off one or two of its blossoms? So often my thoughts seem to be so many shadows twisting, vying against each other for attention within a self-contained, self-perpetuating system of doubt. From this I try to spare you, hoping I might help to make you glad to be alive without always daring to claim such joy for myself – and almost daring to laugh at myself for thinking so ridiculous a thought.

Still, I reflect on this life I've given you and wonder at its worth, at the effects my recurrent melancholy must have on you. Now here again this year, this is not the happy birthday message I had hoped to write you, though again it seems an honest, necessary one. Can you forgive me once more, and shall we answer this apology with an exuberant celebration of these lives we've shared in the face of my many and varied moods?

For an appetizer I've planned the pâté de foie gras we purchased in Paris; for the entrée there's steak rubbed with hickory and marinated in balsamic vinegar and olive oil with bourbon and a quartered sweet onion, then grilled with Parmesan-encrusted potatoes and tomato slices. And we have your favorite Black Forest cake for dessert.

We'll start the cabernet sauvignon, the first tasting of which I'll warm inside my mouth so you can sample its flavors from my lips.

Here's wishing you the happiest of birthdays at thirty-seven, still my favorite number after all these years. May the journey ahead through your thirty-eighth year bring you much happiness, along with all my love.

DecemberSun #10 – *Tops*

Atop our tree this year is Paris, if only in a constellation of postcards. Each year for these past ten, we've drawn upon the inspiration of last-minute whimsy to top our tree with a representative of ourselves, attempting to make personal our observation of this ancient, enveloping season bred of what must be a genetic edict: to celebrate the sun, to celebrate warmth and light even at a time when this northern half of the world is turned furthest from its source.

We have hoisted atop our festive, artful tree a series of our own assertions of light, beginning that first year with a flower you'd made of fur and presented to me, the prototype of the many you were to craft.

The second year an angelic chorister from your past took the flower's place; the third year, drawn from my history, a pair of spiked high heels made of black net with red embroidered roses. In both cases, they were things someone had left behind.

The fourth year we found something natural and new: a bird's nest I'd discovered blown from a grove of Texas live oaks, in which we placed a pair of nesting birds. The fifth year we reiterated the nest, but instead of birds added, erupting from it, a bouquet of dried roses wrapped in lights.

Our sixth year seemed to call for humor; hence a little white bear bent across the top bough, mooning those passing by on the sidewalk below. Atop our seventh tree rode high and proud a pert brown bear waving the rainbow flag acquired at the previous June's Gay Pride Parade.

Our eighth year we drew back to celebrate ourselves with a pair of hand-blown goblets tied fast to each other with satin cords. Last year three doves and a band of light circled an ornament concocted of pipe cleaners by a man we'd met while visiting a friend in a hospital's AIDS ward. He was battling his mortal disease with an infectious cheer and furious creativity.

Now this year we have Paris. My love, our seasons and celebrations turn around central events, events as they are presented to us and as we choose to observe them. I suppose we can't help but wonder how many trees we have left to decorate, how many more times the events of our lives will inspire whimsical commemoration. We're fortunate that we already have this good, healthy stand of memories that will endure. In the joy of celebrating this moment with you now, I feel surrounded already by a dense, old forest. The celebration of life and light which each year has found its symbolic way to the top of our tree is timeless; it's our participation in the ages.

Here's wishing you the best of the season, now and forever, with all my love.

Valentine's Poem

Roses are red, and violets
   Violet.

Goofy sentiment, my love,
 typifies this day of mass-imprinted hearts,
 imposes its silliness on our own deeply serious
   Relationship,
 at the heart of which still beats strong
 that first giddy sensation when we knew.

Tenth Anniversary – *Ten Point Diamonds*

"And perhaps someday to add diamonds, or not."

As it happens, we have. Here in this tenth year of our mating, nestled into each ring there sits a ten-point diamond, another example of serendipitous symbolism discovered *ex post facto*.

Peering through the flat top surface, into the seemingly endless depths of the facets converging at an always-receding point, I wonder what that invisible point might be that so completes these free-flown bands of gold which I first appropriated from you in silver, then gave back to you in gold, which you then returned to me in kind, and whose adornment we've now completed, each with a single diamond whose presence says it's been there from the beginning, just needed time to grow into the open.

I wonder: what piece of wisdom is it that can so fill the one space in the circle of our mating, making it seem so right to leave the other spaces be?

We have a sense of balance about ourselves, don't we? A dynamic, fluid, usually asymmetrical way of setting things about us so that we can take reverie in each individual thing by itself, and in how it combines with others to make a collection. Is it that we do this with ourselves, as well?

I think it's that we seem always to be at once together and apart, our own selves and each other's mate. This is how we are no matter what it is we are doing, so that we make of our separateness another dimension of our closeness. When I retreat within myself, I am aware of how close within me you remain, and I know that when I let you be, I am close within your being as well.

I've observed how a fever or other loss of your body's vitality calls you to attend to your inner self, and I've learned that though I can feel for you, I cannot feel what you feel—nor do you expect me to do so.

I've learned, too, that my own anger, anxiety, hurts, fears, and frustrations are just that—my own. Perhaps the vital lesson we've learned is that we bring our injuries to each other to soothe, not to clone, and that we do nothing to soothe the other's injury by inflicting it upon ourselves. Likewise, we do best for ourselves by taking joy and pride in each other's triumphs without assuming them as our own.

We do not surrender ourselves to each other; rather, we ebb and flow around each other's shores, reconfiguring sands, uncovering treasures, leaving alone landmark monoliths whose mystery we've learned simply to ponder.

We speak intimate words, knowing that when one has said what it is he needs, the other will have heard what it is he's said. With intimate silence, we listen to each other's being with our own, then silently consider whether a response needs to be articulated.

Between us there are no competitions, nor are there judgments. We don't negotiate demands; we integrate the realization of our needs and wishes. We explore, stepping carefully, but knowing that if we'd never taken a wrong turn with each other, we'd know very little of each other's terrain.

It's this knowledge of each other that's allowed us to become not just adult mates, but childhood intimates as well, discovering and wondering aloud about ourselves, our bodies, nature, games, and the whole big world of children and grown-ups around us.

When we play, we share more than a few adult years. We can make up whole new, shared childhoods together from which we then grow up all over again—to be as we are and to love as we love, only some more.

Happy anniversary, my love. May we see these first ten years become happily but a few of the many years to come, I with you, and you with all my love.

Accomplishment

I think of how a day breaks into moments,
 like light into many colors and shadows,
 and I am proud of how well you reckon
 with time's passing as you accomplish your purpose.

Congratulations on your many successes, my love,
 moment by moment, day by day.

Chapter 7: *Vespers* – *Love's Culmination*

Thirty-eighth Birthday – Recognition

Your features are changed this year, your thirty-eighth,
  so that now when I look at you, I am surprised
  yet find I am better able to recognize you,
  your moods, struggles, successes, ambitions, confusions,
  needs, sufficiencies, fears, our interdependencies.

In isolation, drawn apart from a familiar context,
  you become more real to me,
  and I feel more urgently the necessity of us.
  My impulse is to reach for you;
  I want familiarity, the reassurance of touch.

When I see you ill, as has happened often this year,
  what I feel is not pity mistaken for love;
  it's the recognition of a more serious love between us
  than I had imagined in my poetry,
  a love whose proportions are not those of mythic quest
  or romantic ideal, whose impetus is not
  its public or private celebration,
  nor even the banking away of its comfort
  for future recollection.

Instead, it is a quiet, practical matter,
like looking around a room to see what needs to be done.

I like how this more intimate separateness
necessitates questions,
makes me pause to consider what I don't know about you,
informs how I am aware of you.

My hope for this year is that we will share
many a slow, comfortable, surprising embrace.
Happy thirty-eighth birthday, my love,
may we celebrate many another together.

DecemberSun #11 – *by our labors by day and by night, my love*

On this holiday of lights in the too-early dark season,
against winter's stern dictates we again brave cheer,
make delights of our labors to bring to each other,
to please—and ourselves not least of all
then cozy, satisfied, we rest quiet, warm,
stilled from exertion, wondering.

These are not words I give you again,
but my labors by which I have written a complex story
for you to read.

My love, I wish I could make your labors less,
the reading easier, but I cannot with worked-over words
delineate our ambiguous reality.

But remains this hoping, you?
And you.

Here's wishing you the best of this holiday, my love,
with all my love.

Beautiful Moment

With fingers flat, palms open, erect
I touch your buttocks, smooth to press
around my fingers, toward me I pull
from your heat on my skin, I still melt.

I inhale, wrap / grasp / hold my want of you again,
in this beautiful moment, my love,
my sweet valentine,
and again, my love.

Anniversary #11 – *Knowing*

What settles me into us
is how the knowing we have earned of each other
encompasses our unknowns, enabling us
to release ourselves into each other's custody
without hesitation, almost without remark,
knowing as we do what the will of the other holds,
how our holding is accomplished, adapts.

With each next intimacy, my love, may we add
new needs to our knowing, layers

to our comfort in knowing, brave openings
to lifelong conversations.

Happy eleventh anniversary, my love,
 may we celebrate many another together
 I with you, and you with all my love.

Thirty-ninth Birthday –
In Appleton, Again

May you awaken for your birthday amused,
 vital, pleased to live your life each day
 in the place it is.

Would my hand put gently to your face,
 were awakening you here in our home
 alongside the length of me,
 pressed many years close.

Instead, with you away visiting your hometown,
 we maintain the snugness of our fit
 by encompassing the space between us,
 reaching with purpose across this distance
 to touch that which in each other
 creates the first circle of our joy.

Happy thirty-ninth birthday, my love.
 May you find your next year full
 of opportunities for joy,
 and may we both realize them,
 I with you, and you with all my love.

How We Made Love in Paris

You may not know how we made love last night,
 the first of our return to Paris,
 but if you recall

I rubbed your shoulders, the back of your neck,
 your arms, back, buttocks, thighs, calves,
 especially the knotted calves, your ankles, feet and toes,
 each individually, repeatedly,
 with strokes from firm to gentle to whispering,
 seeking to dislodge the jolts set in
 by your wheelchair hauled over cobblestones and up stairs,
 wishing I could likewise work loose
 the encephalopathy from the cells of your brain.

Then, with you asleep, I excused myself
 to stand over the bathroom sink,
 leaving the door slightly open so as to hear
 should you call.

With my hand, slowly at first, in detail,
 then rushing in a whirling collage,
 I remembered other nights in Paris,
 encounters every bit as intimate
 as that just passed.

DecemberSun #12 – *Gifts Given*

My love, on this holiday this year,
 from pieces laid out over eleven holidays past,
 we assemble this present celebration.

We join days with years with care
 to make an intimate embrace
 that carries us through lonely, bewildering moments
 when we know of no other protection.

We spin together our experiences
 with each other's faults, mistakes, and embarrassments,
 then weave of those strands a safety net of humor
 with which we are able to catch one another's falling moods.

From shared needs we construct commitments
 with depth always in excess
 of the breadth of our shifting circumstances.

From our many memories of physical familiarity
 we now pull a voice with which
 one speaks for the other when necessary.
 From the comforts of touch, we produce hope.
 And, by pulling together all that we know or suspect
 of each other, we assemble the essential mystery of our love,
 an intimate and comfortable unknown
 on which we base our complete trust in each other,
 that most valuable of all the gifts we exchange.

Lost Valentine

Sometimes my love wanders in his dreams,
  so, as I sit by his side, I repeat:

"My name is Philip.
  I love you.
  I'll take care of you."

And when he opens his eyes and snorts,
  I'm pleased because he's understood.

Jeffrey never did have a taste for sweets
  so I'm the one left to eat the chocolates,
  which this year I bought bittersweet.

Gifts

Once, when I rubbed too hard while Jeff was seated in our walk-in shower, he shook his finger at me and scolded, "I'm going to tell Philip on you when he gets home!" He didn't always recognize me, but he always knew that there was a Philip looking out for him.

Another time I asked him, "What about all of this bothers you the most?" Gradually, his thinking had become simple, concrete. I wondered if my question was too abstract, but I couldn't bring myself to say "dying". So I said, "all of this". I had to ask, needed to know. Jeff looked me straight in the eye and asked, in reply, "Is your job secure?"

Chapter 8: *Compline – Through the Dark Night*

Letter to Mr. and Mrs. La Londe, Debbie, Reyne, and families

I'm writing to let you know about an experience I had on the morning after Jeff died, which still surrounds me with peace and comfort whenever I think about it, which is often.

As you know, Jeff's wish was to be cremated, for which we had made arrangements. The Cremation Society had come for his body shortly after he died that night. However, I needed to go by their office around ten o'clock that morning to sign the actual authorization papers. My friend Randy had come to be with me through the hours after Jeff's death and had taken the day off work to stay with me.

At 9:45 a.m., as we were preparing to leave, I took my coat from the back of a chair and put it on, somehow in the process knocking over a little silver bear that I'd given Jeff one holiday. Bears, as you know, were Jeff's favorite animals, whereas birds are mine, so each year I'd given him bears, and he'd given me birds. In putting on my coat, I knocked over this bear sitting on the corner of the old sewing machine by the kitchen, and the vibrations from it falling over set off the two mechanical birds on the other side of the machine, one a yellow canary (Jeff's favorite color), and the other a brown and green finch.

You remember how, in response to vibrations, the birds would give just a few chirps? Well, this time the birds started chirping and didn't stop. I picked them up, turned them over, turned off the CD player, held them in my hands, and set them in various locations on the table, and they just didn't stop.

I was flooded with a wonderful sensation of peace and calm and wonder. It didn't seem eerie at all, but just very familiar and beautiful. I thought of various associations such as Jeff's patron saint, St. Francis, preaching to the birds, or of the spoken cantata I'd written for Jeff and how this might be his way of returning it to me. But mostly I just sat holding the birds and feeling the wonderful sensations.

Finally, it got to be after ten o'clock and the birds still hadn't stopped, so I put them in my coat pocket, and Randy and I left to walk up to the Cremation Society. Once outside the building, they did seem to stop, or at least I didn't hear them again until we were in the Cremation Society's office. When the woman started typing information on the forms, the chirping started up again. I looked at Randy, and he looked at me, and we just smiled. Because the birds were in my coat pocket, I think they were quiet enough that the woman behind the desk couldn't hear them, or she might have thought the sound was coming from outside the window.

When we left, I checked the birds and found it was just the canary that was chirping constantly, but that the canary would set off the finch if they were placed next to each other. The canary kept up its chirping through lunch at a restaurant and all the way home. Once we got home, since it was still going strong, I used a screwdriver to open the bird and remove the battery, which made the chirping stop. Inside there was a little piece of loose black electrical tape, which perhaps had something to do with the short-circuit of the shut-off mechanism. But, that's just the mechanical explanation for how the message was delivered.

The timing, symbolism, and the wonderful sensations I experienced convinced me that Jeff was sharing his peace with me.

Once, when I'd asked him what about all that was happening with his health worried him the most, he'd surprised me by asking me in return if my job was secure. I told him I thought so and asked him why. He replied that the thing that worried him the most about dying was that he didn't know how I was going to manage. I think the experience of the birdsong was a gift both to help me manage the immediate task of giving release to his physical body as well as to give me comfort through the difficult times that lay ahead.

I am managing, though it becomes difficult at times as the reality of the separation from him sets in. I know how difficult it is for you, too. I hope by sharing this experience with you I can also share with you some of the peace it's given me. Jeff, meaning "peaceful," was well named. I hope this finds you well, and that your journey here for the memorial service is safe and trouble free.

With warm regards,
Philip.

From *"Elements of Love, a Reader's Cantata*

My love, speak a word, speak open
  my mind gently, the healing begins slowly.
  With you in me, I remember you gone now,
  but speaking.

People, if you would rage against a loss,
  rage creative;
  if you would weep,
  weep with specific intent.

Memorial Remarks

I'd like to thank each of you for coming here today to honor Jeff's memory. He was indeed an inspiration. I look around and see so much that Jeff inspired. I look at your faces and I see loyalty, respect, admiration, friendship, and love. Jeff has become the subject of art, of music, and of literature – and now, too soon, of some of our best memories.

He died too young, and of a disease that lives to claim others. We must accept that fact and respond to it both with creative rage and with soothing tears. One of life's great mysteries is that we must make peace with death when it happens in order to reaffirm our commitment to life.

I hope that coming here today to celebrate Jeff's life, and to mourn his death, will inspire us to live our own lives fully, as did he, and, like Jeff, to take pleasure in being able to help others.

He was a good man. Thank you.

DecemberSun #13 – *Release*

In this DecemberSun season
 I remember a quiet night last spring
 when I gave you my permission to die.

Go to the source, I said.
 I release you from my love
 and give you to all love; I release
 you from my care, and give you
 to the source of all caring; I release
 you from the pain which holds you here
 beyond yourself, so that you may search
 for the mysterious source of all selves.

Go when you must, I said, *I release you*
 from my own secure, familiar hold on you,
 knowing I will hold you even more intimately
 within the space of your absence. My love,

I release you, finally, even from hearing
   the sound of your name carried on my breath,
   lest you mistake it for my beckoning you to stay.
   But know your name, Jeffrey,
   I will always keep resonating within me,
   mingling its sweet-sounding syllables
   with those of my own.

My love, now I need from you a gift
   like that which I gave you last spring:
   as I gave you permission to go,
   from you I need permission to stay.

Shards of your death flow in my blood,
   their sharp jags catching in my veins,
   slicing with violent force at my aorta,
    in my lungs restricting the assimilation
   of new air, cutting short my voice.

Jeffrey, my love, release me, give me tears
   with which to mourn and grieve you, tears
   to celebrate and soothe, secure, reorient,
   stabilize, tears with which to mix a mortar
   to bond these scattered, disjointed emotions
   these memories, perceptions, pieces of life
   into something cohesive, into a memorial wall
   angling into the future that I must live.

My love, let me go on, with all my love.

Intimate Desires
(on our first anniversary postmortem)

Thought:

I want to speak and see my words
  shoot around inside your head,
igniting surprise reactions
  that explode your face into a smile,
Pleased.

Speech:

When my name touches your tongue
I want it to deliver a depth charge
  that resounds between the syllables
and pulls up through your thighs.

Touch:

I want to confide my feelings in looks
  that bring your hands by reflex to follow
along the contours of my moods.

Rhythm:

Playing my fingers across your chest,
  I want to alight on familiar chords,
  then improvise loose variations,
  laying licks and riffs atop your pulsing beat.

Energy:

I want to breathe embedded memories
  of the fragrance of our oils mingling

in the heat from our two bodies rubbing,
skin on skin until incensed.

Thirteenth Anniversary Letter

Jeffrey, my love,

Mourning this morning, I'm surprised with the thought of
how sure I am about how much you loved me, how much I
meant to you. I've recently realized how much I've operated
on the subconscious assumption that life must be a struggle—
an outlook which fueled my frequent bouts of depression and
withdrawal, which had to be exasperating, tedious, even
boring for you, and more than anything, baffling.

I would try to wonder if we were right, healthy for each other,
if what kept us together was truly love, or something more like
a symbiotic, compensatory bonding to protect us from
addressing our insecurities. Unable to accept simple, easy
satisfaction with life, my mind kept trying to find reasons to
dispute our happiness, to find in our joy evidence of our self-
deception. Now I realize that by looking for reasons to
despair, I was creating them. And, in looking through all the
cards and notes you gave me over the years, I realize how
aware you were of this weakness of mine, and how your love
for me surrounded it.

What kept us together was love, that inexplicable, irresistible
attraction we felt to connect our entire beings—known and
unknown—to create an *us* which would wrap our individual
strengths, weaknesses, and secrets around each other's, then

go beyond them to create a complex of interdependencies and self-sufficiency beyond our ability to conceive or analyze.

Whenever I would try to figure out whether we should be together, the answer was always that I just could not conceive of any alternative. There was no potential in the idea of us not being partnered. We connected at levels and at a magnitude beyond anything our conscious minds could consider and decide; the decision was made, remained made by the whole of each of our beings having met.

I am still partnered with you, even now that it has been over a year since your death. *Always* is beginning to mean something real to me now: I will love you always, for so long as I am alive. Perhaps I may have room for other affections, perhaps even another love—I don't know. But you needn't worry that anyone will take your room.

I sense that you know this, that I know this. Somehow the dimensions and physics of the spirit seem to allow for simultaneous rooms, spaces which can occupy the same terrain without impinging upon or diminishing each other's boundaries. That is how I would like to think we lived our lives together, or at least that was the ideal to which we aspired—and more than occasionally managed to achieve, often despite ourselves.

Happy thirteenth anniversary, my love,
  with all my love.

Our Return to the Pacific

September 19, 1998

Site: The beach by Devil's Punchbowl on Oregon's Pacific Coast, just south of Depoe Bay.

I had infused his ashes with his favorite cologne and had mixed into them dried roses from a bouquet I'd given him for our eleventh anniversary. Salt stung my taste buds as the seventh wave of cold ocean water broke and slapped up against my shoulders. I heaved with all my strength, flinging the ashes in an arc toward the sun sitting low on the horizon.

For a moment, the scent of *Gentleman* by Givenchy filled my nostrils as bits of ash flew in my face. The wave grabbed my momentum and toppled me, pushing me toward the shore. As I fell, I let loose the container. When I regained my footing, I retrieved both the container and its inner liner, which had flown free and was floating on the water.

I let the waves wash out all the remains of the ashes, then stood facing the sun, now at virtual eye level. As the waves broke around me, I felt inundated with a sense of peace and reassurance. I knew I had done well by him. Finally, I turned and walked toward the shore.

As I did so, I noticed bits of the dried roses swirling around my legs, suspended between the beach and the sea by the advance and retreat of the waves. When all the bits had finally disappeared, I returned to the beach with the container, dried myself, and dressed.

With a parting look at the sun, which was laying stripes of white light across the surface of the water, I left the beach and climbed the stairs back up to the car.

Appendix – *Chronology*

- Jeff and Phil are assigned to the same Lenten Study Group at Good Shepherd Parish Metropolitan Community Church.

- Jeff blushes at rehearsal for *Lysistrata* at GSP-MCC. After rehearsal they go to Ricky's for bagels and cream cheese.

- They relocate to Fort Worth, Texas for Jeff's training as a furrier.

- Both test HIV+.

- They return to Chicago, where Jeff becomes the fur factory manager.

- Jeff contracts pneumonia. Phil begins writing *Elements of Love*, a semi-autobiographical reader's cantata drawn from his writings for Jeff. Both start AZT.

- *Elements of Love* is performed by NewTown Writers for Gay Pride Week. Jeff begins to experience night sweats and spiking fevers.

- First trip to Paris. They discover the Monet panels at the Musée de l'Orangerie.

- Jeff experiences a retinal artery occlusion, losing partial sight in one eye. Gradually, more frequent— then daily—fevers and sweats follow.

- Jeff quits work, goes on disability.

- Jeff develops his first symptoms of encephalopathy.

- Jeff develops CMV, loses sight in one eye. He's in a wheelchair due to advancing encephalopathy, is recommended to the hospice program.

- Return trip to Paris to see Monet panels.

- Jeff dies around 2:00 a.m. at home, attended by Phil.

- Memorial service.

- Phil scatters Jeff's ashes in the Pacific Ocean.

Book 3

Bliss: A Marriage Proposal

for Charles Stephen Hughes, presented to him on 6/24/2012

A collection of poetry, prose, and paintings
which culminate in a marriage proposal, private in nature
but made public here for all to read
because the personal is still political

Chapter 1 –

Our Beginning

Exciting the Poet –
The Night We Met

I am not promiscuous about writing poetry, so it was significant that after our first meeting, which was also our first night together, I wrote a set of four poems for my current partner, Charles Stephen. I'd written pieces regularly for my previous partner, Jeff, but in the four years since his death I had only once written a poem for a living person. Coincidentally, that poem was also for someone named Charles, and the occasion was also our having slept together – though that time was in our underwear, without touching.

That isn't how it was with Charles Stephen.

The first Charles was a young man who, like me, did volunteer work at a group home serving people who were impacted by AIDS and in need of housing. He spoke eloquently of his vegan philosophy, lifestyle, and diet, and I was taken with his quiet, comprehensive devotion to his way of life. He was the first vegan with whom I'd had lengthy, mellow conversation. I think he enjoyed playing the role of teacher to someone significantly older.

We slept together just once. We'd been out at an event later than planned, and it wasn't practical for him to drive all the way to his home only to be back within a few blocks of my apartment to work a shift early the next morning. I was amused at the lengths to which he went to keep the experience pristine.

Someday, when Charles Stephen is looking through my various writings dedicated to him, he may be puzzled to discover an unfamiliar one marked "for Charles." Reading it, he'll wonder, *"When did we ever sleep together in our underwear?"*

From our very first night together, Charles Stephen and I have always shed our underwear upon getting under the covers. This is not to say, however, that we were totally unrestrained from the get-go. "No sex on the first date," he told me, stopping my head as it was working its way down his chest toward his erect penis. I thought it endearing that he should impose this rule at that point—endearing, and a little unfair, considering that his lips had just wrapped around my own erect penis, albeit briefly.

But he insisted, and I had to respect the rule. Touch but don't taste. I didn't know if he was being coy just with me, or if this was a standard rule for him. I took it to mean, in either case, that he probably wanted to see me again, that I wasn't a one-night stand. That pleased me immensely, as I'd very much enjoyed our chance meeting and the fun evening of laughter, dancing, and conversation that had ensued.

I'd stopped into The Granville Anvil, a small neighborhood gay bar about a block away from my apartment in the Artist in Residence complex around 11:00 p.m. on the evening of November 14, 1998. I was on my way home from a dance concert and felt like having a quick libation before going to bed. There wasn't anything to drink at home, but I didn't feel like getting on the El to go down to the bars in Boys Town either. I didn't want to carouse the night away; I just wanted a quiet drink and then to be home, in bed by midnight. Alone, presumably.

I'd only stopped into The Granville Anvil a couple of times over the three years I'd lived in the neighborhood. I'm not much of one to socialize in bars. For one thing, my hearing is such that I have difficulty distinguishing voices if there are multiple sound sources: loud music, conversations, televisions. On the rare occasions I go to a bar by myself, I mostly just sit and watch people. If someone speaks to me, I nod in agreement, but usually I haven't a clue what they've said. You could count the number of times I've been picked up in a bar on your hands and still have plenty of fingers left to hold your drink. And I've never initiated a pick-up.

That night, the bar was as I'd remembered it, nothing fancy, just a neighborhood meeting place. A moderately lit, large island bar circled on three and a half sides by barstools. More people, almost all male, than the times I'd been in previously, but still a few empty seats. The walls held an accumulation of things: an advertising mirror, a theatrical poster, a reproduction of a landscape oil painting, an odd modernist painting on plywood—perhaps bartered to pay off a tab?

Bland gay pornography played on the TV sets hanging at either end of the room. The air smelled of beer and cigarette smoke.

I headed toward an empty stool at the far end of the bar and sat down between two men. Both were of medium build and appeared about ten years younger than me. The man on my left immediately smiled and introduced himself as "Charles." This was not the Charles whom I knew from my volunteer work. The man on my right seemed oblivious, absorbed in his own thoughts. I ordered a beer and focused on the animated, flirtatious Charles.

The jukebox was playing, so I tried to read his lips and hear what I could. We managed to exchange some conversation. I told him I was working on my master's in interdisciplinary arts. He joked about always wanting to meet someone in the *disciplinary* arts. He said he was artistic as well—did drawings, maybe choreography; I don't remember exactly. I missed a lot because he often turned to talk to others. Still, he kept returning to me, and after a fashion, we chatted.

After a few awkward pauses, I explained my hearing difficulty. From then on, whenever he caught me looking blank, he'd seductively lean so his lips were right at my ear and repeat himself in deep, conspiratorial tones. One or both of his hands usually landed on my thigh for support when he did this. Perhaps I was misinterpreting, as older gay men sometimes do when younger ones pay them attention, but I had the distinct feeling I was on the menu.

Then a swarthy, stocky man in an orange plaid flannel shirt and red cap entered the front door. Charles stopped mid-sentence, dashed to him, and soon returned with him in tow. Charles told me this was Chris, a cheese farmer from Wisconsin. Charles told Chris that I was a nice guy, a fellow artist. It was clear my plate had been pulled from the menu. Amused but undeterred, I finished my beer, planning to head home.

That's when the quiet man on my right finally spoke:

"So you're an artist, and you live in that building around the corner, Artist in Residence?"

I hadn't realized he'd been paying attention. Smiling pleasantly, he extended his hand.

"My name is Stephen," he said. "Charles Stephen, actually, but I just use Charles at work. My friends all call me Stephen."

"Nice to meet you, Stephen," I replied, looking into a pair of eyes that instantly aroused my poet. I waved for another beer and leaned back on my stool. What followed was animated conversation, a trip to another nightclub to dance, sitting on his lap when an old date awkwardly stopped by, and finally a slightly tipsy walk to my apartment through the crisp November night air – two men laughing, full of anticipation.

One Good Morning

Now one decade ago
  after a night of bliss
  I awoke to the expectation
  that our history had begun.

We went about it in the usual way:
  brunch, our stories,
  exchanging phone numbers. I said
  I'd call; you didn't expect I would.

The next day I did, to your delight.
  Then, emboldened, I drew my pen
  and wrote four little poems—
  just enough to get us started.

For ten years now, we've gone about
  making our history in the usual ways:
  together putting our home together,
  then together helping you rearrange it,
  going to our jobs, coming home,

  happily soothing each other's nerves,
  curling up for naps, massaging feet,
  pursuing art and music, paying bills,
  putting on pounds, growing grey hair.

Our lives may not be extraordinary,
  but what I feel for you each day
  feels extraordinary, feels epic, feels

like the center of my life, feels
like our history, just getting started.

The First Four:

Revelation

Yours is a face I can see
 speaks truth,
 even as it hides
 a surprise nip on my lip
 as I close in for a kiss.

Tease

His skin like milk chocolate,
 melting in my hand becomes slick
 with passion. I grab the round muscles
 of his butt and squeeze hard.

He spasms and yelps. We roll naked
 around the bed, pulling our bodies
 into ever new configurations
 of intimate contact.

Briefly his lips
 play havoc on my erection.
 I lean my head toward his own
 quivering cock. He closes his legs.

No sex on our first date,"
he whispers.

Reflection

Waking to the back of your head
nestled in the crook of my arm,
I gaze at the tightly textured black curl
and feel a familiar peace reinstated
a quiet exhilaration of joy that runs
the length of my body touching yours.

Naughty Boy's Birthday

Mr. Scorpio Man likes to sting
with little surprises: languid,
gentle strokes, then a pinch;
soft lips on nipples suddenly bite.

Mr. Scorpio Man likes to earn
his birthday swats.

(Our first meeting was four days prior to Stephen's birthday.)

Chapter 2 – *All About You*

Stephen, my love

When we met, I fell in love with the boy in your eyes, your willingness to follow some wild impulse all the way home. With you I knew I could be bold and dare to be my unguarded self. You are still every bit, and more, the boy I first met, but now, having lived with you, I've come to love and respect the man you are as well. From you I've learned that to be a better person, I just need to be more myself.

You read people's spirits, mine and those of others. Your entertainment is in sharing the news about what people say and do, but you don't judge. Your insight into the values and valuables that people hold within them is keen. You forgive foibles—indeed, you delight in them with an enthusiasm that only a true lover of humanity can exude.

You handle adversity well. You accept setbacks but never defeat. When faced with loss or disappointment, you regroup quickly and plan for a better tomorrow. You'll own up to your errors, but you will not let them possess you.

You are your own man, and if the mood strikes, your own woman, too. Whatever the circumstances or consequences, you hold true to the person you know yourself to be—even if that means you have to talk fast to get yourself out of a tight spot.

You have many complexities and many simple delights. With you I feel grateful to be alive, and proud to say you are my mate.

Happy thirty-seventh birthday, my love. May the years continue to enrich you,
with all my love.

Hey Mr. Man

Hey Mr. Man, Mr. Badassed Queen, says he's from New Orleans Man...

Hey Mr. Elegant, Mr. Hunky, Mr. Spirit-of-a-beautiful-woman Man...

Hey Mr. Coos "Honeysweetcomelovemesomemore" Man...

Hey Mr. Naughty nips-at-my-tits-in-the-middle-of-making-love, Mr. Wants-me-to-swat-his-ass-hard, taught-me-how Man...

Hey Mr. Scorpio-in-the-ninth-house, feels people's spirits and knows whenever I'm thinking something I'm not saying Man...

Hey Mr. Righteous, always testifying to his riches as a child of the Heavenly Father who watches over us, provides for us, and gives us no more than we can bear Man...

Hey Mr. "Oh no she did NOT go THERE with me, I will read her, I will beat her down, I will cut her, I can be a bad motherfucker so she best don't be messin' with me, I will talk this shit but wouldn't never do nobody no harm" Man...

Hey Mr. Doesn't-like-to-be-called-beautiful-but-doesn't-mind-gorgeous, though he doesn't think he is, just stands at the mirror and says he doesn't look cute today, has to brush his hair and pound his face some more but says "I'm ready to go" (pulls out the make-up bag)... says "I'm ready to go" (sorts through the cologne bottles)... says "I'm ready to go" (changes his earrings)... says "I'm ready to go" (bends over to pull on his socks) Man...

Hey Mr. Charles Stephen, aka Stephen, aka Charles, aka Steve, Stevie, Charlie, Chuck, Chuckie, Beaver, Edward (your mother told me) Hughes, Junior (it's on your birth certificate) Man...

Hey Mr. Man of my dreams, perfect for me in every way, delights me, intrigues me, makes me feel happy, makes me feel sexy, makes me feel glad to be alive, makes me feel complete trust Man...

Hey Mr. Man, my man, will you be my Valentine, maybe for a long, long time?

With all my love,

Stephen, my love

I cannot fully describe with words
how contemplating the fact of you
holds my world together, makes me
giddy with delight. With you I live
inside feelings at once familiar
and baffling, never knowing
what new facet of you I will discover
amid an ordinary conversation
or lurking beneath a kiss.

With each exaltation of song
you shout to the heavens
while mopping the kitchen floor,
each search through secret potions
on the shelves of drugstores
and beauty boutiques, each scolding
you give me correcting my life,
each whim-driven shopping spree,
each rearrangement of home décor
you surprise me in a way
that in another way doesn't.

When you wrap your arms familiar,
like magic, around me you create home,
family, the first circle of my life,
holding strong to the bond we give
of ourselves to each other, faithful
to the complete trust we hold
that each wants for the other

only that which enriches our life,
sustains our love.

Happy Anniversary, my love,
with all my love.

Your Birthday List

"I love you," I said.

"Why?" you asked.

"For so many reasons," I replied,
 "that I can't begin to name them."

"I want a list," you said.

Very well, my love, here then, for your birthday, is the list:

- I love you because nothing about you is bland.
- I love you because you will go from being a little brat boy to a grand diva and back before I can finish a breath.
- I love you because your creativity manifests in all that you do.
- I love you because you like to see yourself looking good.
- I love you because you love to cuddle.
- I love you because you are so open to finding joy in life.
- I love you because you are so willing to invest so much of yourself into any chosen project, whether that be

cleaning the house or producing an album of original songs.

- I love you because every so often you'll insist I laze away a day with you in bed.
- I love you because you believe in yourself and your abilities, and aren't afraid to attempt anything you decide you want to accomplish.
- I love you because you don't dwell on setbacks.
- I love you because you choose your friends carefully, are loyal to them, emphasize their attractions, accept their flaws, and are always willing to defend them.
- I love you because you believe in me and my potential, because I hear you praise me to your friends.
- I love you because you are always respectful of me.
- I love you because you have a realistic acceptance of my shortcomings and don't hold them against me.
- I love you because I know I can trust you to choose for yourself whatever is best for us.
- I love you because every day of living with you reminds me anew of all of the reasons why I love you, and more often than not reveals even more.

Happy Birthday, my love,
with all my love.

An Advent Calendar of Word Gifts

Jubilation

because you love to discover joy anywhere it can be found,
  and are so adept at it.

Honesty

because you open your mind, body, and soul to me.

Acumen

because you learn quickly and comprehend complexities.

Steadfast

because you always recognize who I am to you
  and treat me with esteem.

Reverence

because of your inner sense of what's holy
  and your deep devotion to it.

Elegance

because you convey style wherever you go
  and in whatever you do.

Commitment

because you will give of yourself without reservation.

Inventiveness

because your mind is creative, quick, and surprising.

Stature

because you command respect from all who know you.

Compassion

because you stop to think about how people feel
  and can feel with them.

Amiability

because you invite friendliness in the people you meet.

Orientation

because you know your direction and your destination.

Playfulness

because of your youthful exuberance
 and your love of fun.

Vigor

because of your energetic devotion to work and play.

Emotive

because you feel deeply
 and express your feelings fully.

Tranquility

because you allow your presence
 to soothe and mellow frayed nerves.

Spontaneity

because you are open to the unexpected.

Loyalty

because you measure friendships
 in decades of trust.

Honor

because you recognize and respect your conscience.

Authenticity

because you speak your own words
 with your own voice.

Curiosity

because your mind is always ready to grow.

Appreciation

because you recognize others
 for what they bring to your life.

Discipline

because you will work for what you want.

Benevolence

because your presence in my life
 is a most cherished gift.

Love

Because in a word
 I celebrate your presence with me again this day
 when we celebrate the birth of love made human,
 made holy all it touches,
 as made manifest in your hand
 softly put to my face.

With all my love,

Finding Delight

I delight in your ability
 to live life fully, in the wonder
 you take in discovering
 a good bowl of soup
 or a juicy piece of gossip.

I delight in your Aunt Flo walk
the sturdy swish of your hips
like that of a wise, strong woman
who has seen a lot of life
and understood it.

I delight in the soft curl of your back
as you cuddle against me in bed,
the soft, smooth feel of your flesh
as you tuck your whole big body
inside the little, embracing cavern
of my arms and legs.

I delight in your music, your voice
as you shout your soul's deliverance
so loudly that surely the angels
not to mention the neighbors
must share the rapture of your gospel.

I delight in the kindness you show me,
your patient tolerance
of my big artistic tantrums
and little boy crimes
(sneaking a cigarette with your mom).

I delight in loving you, watching you
inhabit our home, feeling your presence
even when we're apart
and I delight in knowing you
find your delight in me, too.

Attack of the Oil-Based Enamel Black Paint

The weekend before last, Macy's had a bed-in-a-bag sale. Stephen researched their inventory online for hours and finally decided on just the right set to complement everything else we had going on in our bedroom. He woke up very early Saturday morning to be at Macy's doors when they opened at 9 a.m. He returned late Saturday afternoon with the news that the set he'd wanted was not in stock and would no longer be available. He'd settled on another set, a gold, patterned one which he thought would work, but which might require some adjustment to the room to harmonize.

The rest of the day, reaching into the wee hours of the morning, was spent making unsatisfying adjustments: different rugs, different artwork, different furniture, etc. Alas, Sunday morning it was off to Bed, Bath and Beyond for another bed-in-a-bag, this one a solid burgundy, which required further adjustments throughout the week.

What became clear while attempting to make the adjustments, however, was that the problem really wasn't with the bedspread. The problem, it turns out, was that the chair that we'd been using at the desk was just irredeemably all wrong for the room. So, this past weekend he came home from Pier One with an intricately woven, huge rattan chair, so huge, in fact, that there is no way we can possibly fit it at the desk. Never mind, we'll get out the step stool and sit on that whenever we want to work at the desk.

The chair can occupy the other corner of the room once the clothes hamper, floor lamp, and my art supplies are removed to the basement. We now have a duffle bag in the closet where we deposit our dirty clothes, which functions well enough. And no, we needn't worry about our clean clothes absorbing odors from being in an enclosed space with dirty laundry because the bag is constructed of very heavy canvas.

The size of the chair, however, threw off all the proportions in the room, and virtually everything except for the bed, the desk, and the dresser had to be removed. My figure drawings above the dresser no longer worked, so I was commissioned to create three new abstract pieces on Sunday, using burgundy.

Once I had finished these by Sunday evening, it was obvious that every frame in the house should be painted black. Presciently, it happened that he'd purchased some black paint when he was out buying the second bed in a bag. Monday evening, as I set about preparing dinner, he covered the sofa, throw rug, and television in our very small back room with a plastic drop cloth and set up shop. I'd suggested waiting for a weekend, and perhaps working in the basement, but he didn't think that necessary.

Just as I was bringing the rice to a boil, I heard an urgent, plaintive call for me to bring a wet cloth and a pan of water. I quickly did so, whereupon I discovered that he'd not removed the Plexiglas and artwork from the frames before painting them, nor had he taped off the edges of the Plexiglas. Being a more vigorous than delicate painter, black paint was now all over the Plexiglas, and he urgently wanted to wipe it off before it dried.

Without thinking I handed him the wet rag, though my reptilian brain said *no*. As he began to wipe, or rather, smear the paint, I looked at the paint can and confirmed that it read **oil-based black enamel.** I'd recognized the odor. He was certain he'd purchased latex. At this point there were already drips of long-drying, sticky black paint all over his pants, his hands, and the plastic covering the room.

I told him not to move and quickly went to the basement to retrieve the turpentine I use for my oil paints. As he cleaned his hands, I cleaned the paint off the Plexiglas.

Well, since I already had the paint thinner, there was no reason not to proceed. As I fretted over preparing the rest of dinner, suggesting a time or two that he wait until I could help, he tore apart the frames, removed the artwork and Plexiglas, reassembled the frames, and went at them with the paintbrush. Somehow, he managed to paint eight frames sized 24"x32" or larger and fit them around each other on the plastic tarp to dry inside this very small back room, all without asphyxiating either of us on the fumes.

By Tuesday evening they were dry, mostly, so as I again fretted over dinner, he returned the artwork to the frames and returned the frames to the walls without leaving all that many spots. We've yet to pick up the plastic, but if there is black enamel paint on the sofa, TV, or floors, there's not a lot, and it wasn't put there intentionally, so that absolves that.

Three frames remain to be painted, but he has suggested we
wait for a weekend to attack them, and perhaps do so in the
basement. I agreed—because that's what I truly love about
him: his uncanny ability to precisely discern the outermost
stretch of my overextended nerves.

On Your 39th

For this, your very first
thirty-ninth birthday
I wish you many happy returns
on the investment you make
every day in your bed-rocking belief
that life is to be thoroughly enjoyed.

I hope that I will always return to you
the reassurance you give me
that the joy we find in each other
and our lives together
will always by far exceed
any worry that comes our way.

Love is always life's best argument
against despair, a case you make
with the kind of laughter that speaks
of your irrefutable love for life
in all its many shades and colors,
in all its many passages of light and shadow,
in all its whispers and shouts and songs
flowing fresh from your soul.

Happy 39th birthday, my love,
with all my love.

Knowing You

No matter how often
 or in how many ways
 you declare your love for me,
 I am always taken
 by how fresh and honest
 you make the words sound.

You have a gift
 for saying what you feel,
 for feeling what you feel
 with simple purity,
 without doubt,
 without reservation.

You know yourself
 without being self-absorbed.
 You are self-aware
 without being self-conscious.
 And should you be surprised,
 your response is always self-assured.

Knowing you,
 I can't always know
 what's coming next,
 but I can know
 that whatever it is,

it will be authentic,
and meant to benefit us.

Happy Birthday, my love,
with all my love.

My Type of Man

If you could remain
  as trustworthy as you are,
  as vivacious as you are,
  as full of fun and mischief,
  as intelligent and expressive,
  as musical and charismatic,
  as devoted to my well-being,
  as carefully groomed,
  elegant and stylish,
  as compassionate and empathetic,
  as concerned for others,
  as generous and thoughtful,
  as protective of our home,
  as engaging with our friends,
  as much in love with life,
  and in love with me,
  as you are

  and have thighs
  a bit more slender,
  say, like a swimmer's,

then perhaps you would be
more my type.

But probably not.
I've come to love your thighs.

With all my love.

Face to Face

When you look into a mirror,
 so often you see a project
 requiring mud packs and ointments,
 a landscape to design for presentation,
 a garden to moisturize and groom.

Do you not realize the real secret
 to your arresting beauty
 lies in the humanity you express
 through each feature of your face,
 every day in your engagement with life?

When reading the faces of strangers,
 I always reference your own.
 Do their eyes reveal perception
 as keen as it is compassionate?
 Do they radiate a light
 that reflects their joy with life?
 How much effort would be needed
 to shape their lips into a smile?

Is their visage relaxed,
not struggling to hide secrets?

The vital architecture of your face
invites people to be at their ease
in the company of a good friend,
taking in your fresh, honest air,
basking in the light and warmth
of someone ready to listen,
ready to laugh at an absurdity,
ready to gently soothe one along
toward hope for a better day.

Happy Valentine's Day, my love,
with all my love.

About You, Mister

If I answer
the playful inquiry of a friend
that yes, you are uncut,
I am in trouble
because that's private,
nobody's business
(and certainly nothing to write about!)

Yet later I overhear you
on the phone,
taking delight in telling friends
how I like
to lick your balls.

Are there rules
 for these rules?
 Instructions on how they apply?

You'll spend hours
 talking on the phone
 but rarely will deign
 to answer it when it rings.

Your fierce loyalty
 to your friends
 is matched only by
 your proclivity
 to gossip about them.

You'll stand for an hour
 in front of a mirror
 in order to perfect
 the most casual of appearances.

You'll tear up the house
 in a rush to leave,
 yet stop repeatedly to view
 front, back, and both sides
 each and every time
 a new piece of attire is donned.

On any given Saturday
 you may rise early
 to clean the apartment
 like a hell-bent housekeeper
 gone righteous mad.

Then, like a shopper
  even more madly driven,
  leave and traverse the city,
  trailing a whim for hours,
  only to return home
  exhausted but ready
  to empty the closets
  and prepare for hours
  to go out to party
  late into the night.

OR, instead

you may lie lethargic
  all day long in bed, awake
  but lifeless into the wee hours
  of Sunday morning, watching TV.

How is it you'll pour yourself
  for months on end
  into creating your music,
  then forbid me to mention it
  much less play it
  for anyone but us,
  for fear it's not exactly right,
  as you confess to friends
  that *I'm such a perfectionist?*

Such is the logic of your quirks.
  Are they to be examined,
  or are they best left alone,
  simply to be enjoyed?

I love your quirks.
And I love that you
love me completely
for all of my quirks as well.

Happy Birthday, my love,
with all my love.

Wrinkle Cream

Sometimes at an evening's end,
I'll watch the intimate story of you
as told in your drooping eyes, at once
those of a child still fighting sleep
despite being already soundly situated
well within its folds, and at the same time
those of a wizened elder, a man settled
into all that he has known and seen
in a life seasoned with frequent laughter.

Of course, you are at present
neither young nor old. Instead, you are
of middle age, still able to deny
with a single dab of specialized cream
a wrinkle's ill-advised encroachment
upon your face's well-defended terrain.

Still able to allow assumptions
that readily delete a dozen years or more
from the well-moisturized record
of your preemptively flawless skin.

Yet I wonder about those transparent years,
equal in length to how long you've known me.
Have I left no telltale mark, no impression?
Can people not look at you and know
that I have been there?

Or perhaps I, too, am like the wrinkle cream,
able to arrest your aging process
with a single, specialized kiss,
a dab of lip balm to ameliorate
the visible advance of age.

Yes, my love, I believe I do possess that power:
to remove years, to rejuvenate your appearance,
to grant you an eternal fountain of youth,
if not in the mirror, then certainly in my eyes.

Happy Valentine's Day, my ever-young love,
with all my love.

After the Argument

My drama diva
gets giddy with glee
when he pisses me off,
then becomes an ice princess
when I want to discuss
what happened.

He gives me a cold shoulder
and the silent treatment,

neither of which
I am allowed to touch
with either words or caresses.

Instead I must endure
my isolation,
usually until sometime
around mid-morning
of the next day,
when he will break his silence
to inform me that I am loved
after all, despite my flaws.

Unless, of course,
I write him a poem
like this one
in which case
I will probably be cut off
for at least a month.

With all my love.

A Birthday Gratitude

Do you wonder why
I love to look at you?

Why, as you nap,
or brush your teeth,
or iron your clothes

Why in ordinary moments
so often you catch me
gazing at you,
absorbed in thought?

When you present yourself
to others, a completed picture,
perfectly groomed and dressed,
I feel great pride for you,
am amazed I have been chosen
to be publicly declared your mate,

But it's at home, un-primped,
going about our daily routines,
that I most often recognize,
stop, and contemplate
the many blessings
you bring to my life.

Thank you, my love,
for bringing me to another happy birthday.
I look forward to sharing many more with you,
with all my love.

I Love How You Are
Your Music

I love how, when you sing,
  your joy takes wing to soar our minds free,
  free for the moment
  of lower atmospheric concerns:
  time, stamina, and finance,
  those ancient and forever recurrent fogs
  which regularly roll across
  our civilized, mortal terrain.

Your music is enlivened light,
  your love of it a pure passion
  that radiates like a rising sun
  setting fire to clouds
  hanging low in the eastern sky.

When you perform for me,
  I am an auditorium filled with energized fans,
  barely able to contain ourselves.
  We are unbound, ablaze, euphoric.

We believe in telepathic flight,
  in the widened expanse of our vision
  of what's possible.

We will not, cannot,
  exist for long at this height,
  yet the glow awakened by having been here,

and the promise of our return
to its full splendor, will sustain us.

It will transform many a seemingly mundane task
into a stage on which we will reenact our elevation,
enlist others in our transgression of the dictate
that we live ordinary lives.

You, your music sets me free.

With all my love.

My Man of Joy

My love, in my sleep I whisper "I love you"
as you dream joy into being.

During the day your laughter ignites
chain reactions of joy exploding
in the psyches of all who hear it.

The glee with which you greet people
irradiates away every glum,
sorry molecule within sight of it.

Your smile bears gospel witness
to the power of joy
to lift the soul into living
a better day, a better life.

Your gift is that you are a transmitter of joy.
Are you surprised that the exuberance

of your spirit captivates passers-by
so that some just stare?

Be kind, they don't mean to be rude.
It's that the strength of your stride,
the uplifted focus of your vision,
the glow which emanates from all around you
pulls at their own buried possibilities for joy
within their own lives.

People aren't always familiar with that feeling,
don't know what to make of it,
whether or not to trust it.

I hope that you will encourage them,
give them a little smile,
a wink or a nod in passing.
Leave them with some positive reinforcement
to discover and grow their own glowing presence.

My birthday wish for you is that you will always be grateful
for this powerful gift,
that you will remain aware and respectful
of its effect on people,
and that it will prove its own reward
as the joy that you give others
continually increases your own.

Happy Birthday, my love, my man of joy.
Here's hoping that I will always be able to give you
the kind of joy that I feel whenever I see your face
light up a room.

Happy Birthday, my love.
With all my love.

After the Interview

In your business attire
 you look to me
 like you could own the world.

But you need not wear a suit and tie
 for me to see your success.

All you need to do is to smile
 one of your smiles that says
 your life is rich in appreciation
 for the dance of life.

Congratulations, my love,
 on another successful day
 of just being yourself
 and doing it so well.

With all my love.

Triumph

Fierce and proud,
 with dignity preserved,
 is a look you wear well
 as is hopeful and unbowed.

You claim victory
 by looking beyond
 the immediate outcome
 of any given battle.

You prevail
 by looking beyond
 the evil done you
 to the good in store.

You succeed
 by living your life
 as one that befits a champion,
 at ease with his honor.

Happy Birthday, my love,
 with all my love.

On Turning Forty

What sort of gift
 would become you
 as you become forty?

You have good will,
 loyalty and kindness,
 intelligence, respect,
 confidence and wisdom.

You have a presence
 that attracts good people,

joy with life, compassion,
generosity and optimism.

You have an eye for beauty,
a talent for self-expression,
a democratic affinity
for the wide palette of life.

You have a ready smile,
a genuine, hearty laugh,
appreciation for life's absurdities,
tolerance for people's foibles.

You have a spirit
that's slow to take offense,
and an understanding heart
that readily forgives.

You have certainty
in your beliefs,
flexibility in their application,
assurance of love
both human and divine.

Already you possess
all that you need
to make your life happy,
to make your life a success.

What more can I give
but my love and amazement,

my adoration for all that you are
and all that you give me?

Happy fortieth birthday,
my love, with all my love.

Here's to HUES — A Gentleman's Delight

Chas. Stephen's HUES embodies the fragrance of
sensuous, polished masculinity.

The first whiff is that of an early, 4:15 a.m. rising
with self-determination and focused energy
drawn from a carefully composed morning regimen
of earthy clays and an array of refreshing scents
plucked from garden, orchard, and rainforest.

Count among these:
cucumber watermelon, eucalyptus bamboo,
luscious sweet fig, ginger mandarin, rain-kissed leaves,
green tea, pear, caramel pear, apple acacia,
lavender citrus, almond shea, and apricot,
all layered atop the aroma of smooth, freshly-showered skin,
warm to the touch and lightly wrapped
in a newly laundered, all-cotton, terrycloth towel.

Mix with this the air of facial topographies ranging
from the perfectly smooth-shaven, so admired by women,
to the five o'clock shadow of stubble, so appealing to men.

Then combine all of the above with the aroma
of classic, relaxed, yet chic couture and impeccable grooming,
a smile that says he's delighted to see you,
and a conversational style that proves it.

Add a knowing glint in the corner of mischievous eyes.

Many may desire, but only the most fortunate
is able to get inside this alluring scent,
to experience its provocatively warm, minty breath
exhaled across moist, full lips
to inhale its mélange of olfactory delights
luxuriously simmered in passion,
then heated to the point of eruption,
blasting one's nostrils with a manly aroma
that rivets one to its source.

***Chas. Stephen's HUES*, for the truly discerning
gentleman's delight.**

Happy Birthday, my love,
with all my love.

Chapter 3 – *Getting Cozy*

Hypnotist

Exhale slowly
 your warm, humid breath
 wafts languorously
 over my mouth,
 mesmerizing my lips
 open to your suggestion.

With all my love,

Four-Posted Footplay

First, we'll light a candle for your every year, birthday boy,
 and station them on stands around our four-posted bed.

Then we'll lay your freshly showered body naked
 across the sheets, giving me free access to your feet.

I'll place my tongue flat on one heel
 and trail a lick up along the line of the arch,
 then repeat the sensation on the other foot.

My lips will envelop each toe
 and gently suck it into the chamber of my mouth;

I'll curl my tongue down between each digit
and ever so gently pull my lower incisors
up over the soft under-face.

Massaging your calves with my hands,
I'll kiss and lick and nip a wild dance
over the entire surface of each foot,
from underside to topside to ankle to arch to heel to toe
and back again until you groan for relief.

Then I'll bite hard on the thickened skin
of the walking surface,
until you scream with delight.

To finish you off, I'll blow dry the sensitized wet flesh
with my warm breath,
while using the very tips of my fingers
to trace a thousand wispy lines
from your straining ankles
to the very excited tips of your toes.

When I suddenly stop and you open your eyes,
you'll see me poised to proceed
with the rest of this birthday massage.

Happy Birthday, my love,
with all my love.

Caveman

Asleep,
  you reach for me,
  both arms extended.

One hand
  encounters my head,
  grabs onto my hair,
  and pulls.

I slide
  into your strength,
  pressing my back
  against your chest.

Your other hand
  scrubs my hip,
  then comes to rest,
  cupping my crotch.

With your breath
  steady and hot
  on the nape of my neck,
  I lie there and dream
  of primitive ravages
  I hope might ensue.

With all my love,

How Our Lady Plays

"Boo! Hiss! Boo!
I say to you, mister.
Now you may, if you wish,
kiss me."

This I endure every night.
The lady plays hard to get,
Throws taunts and teases
which I toss off
or on occasion toss back
to his delighted outrage
until at last,
either he abdicates
and pulls me to him,

or I decide, by brute force,
to overcome his resistance
by wrapping myself around him,
tenderly but firmly engulfing
his mock struggles,
until whimpering he whispers:
"I give up, you have me."

Happy Birthday, my love.
Here's hoping we share
many, many more years together,

before our game ends
as a tie that holds forever.

With all my love,

How I Know You

I know you by the scent of your testicles
against my nostrils, the taste of your tender,
rose-puckered anus scrubbed clean enough
for me to eat out with delight. I know you
by the sweet, dark salt of your perspiration,
the ache in my body when we're like this in bed.

I know you by the slick, warm, liquid velvet
of your lips enveloping my penis, by the moan
that escapes your throat when my fingers
gently probe your prostate. Then I know you
by the shudder of your body when my fingers
pinch your nipples, by the arch of your back
when I bite your broad shoulders or put my teeth
to your biceps. I know you by the taste
of your saliva as your marauding tongue takes
whatever it can reach in my mouth.

I know you by the teasing it takes to pull up the semen
from the depths of your sex and make you blow it
across your belly like a banquet set for my consumption.
I know you by the electric, expansive jolt you trigger
which skews me away from all conscious thought
and melts my body into liquid, undulating waves

that splatter across your chest. Then I know you
by the warm huddle of seamless flesh we become
as we drift to sleep in each other's arms, secure
in our knowledge of each other.

My love, may we continue to know each other
for a very, very long time.
With all my love.

My only drawing from Stephen as a model. He refused future
sessions because he though I'd drawn his thighs too large.

Chapter 4 — *What You Do to Me*

Bliss

I ease into the fragrant,
 freshly drawn bath of your music
 like love, sensual, cleansing, accepting.
 The warmth of your voice radiates deep,
 my muscles relax, release concerns
 and consternations dissolve like salts,
 soothing my mind settles into your love,
 like music, reinvigorates my life.

With all my love.

Like Persimmons

Mellow, luscious,
 plump with years and silken ripe
 each kiss, each glance, each embrace
 harvested, chosen and plucked:
 a gift from nature, filled with the sweet juice
 of our shared history.

Happy anniversary, with all my love.

A River Side by Side Flows

Smooth, my fingers caress tender across your familiar skin,
pressed intimate on my own dreams in passionate colors
they swirl with emotions deep-rooted beneath words like love
surface daily like your warm breath on my lips after a kiss.

Entangle our arms, embrace our history melts remembered
into years repeating themes deepen in resonance: the sound
of each other's name to our ears, complex and well-known
ripples of sound we travel daily from slumber's subconscious
terrain to our waking, aware of presence.

Sanctified, this bond renews as routine expressions
of kindness; tenderness floods around our lives; we wrap
layers of comforting accumulate by degrees to on occasion
ignite instinct-laden drives manifest in flesh honored
expressions of our divine desire to mate.

Your promise, held cherished in my mind, realizes again
each day steadfast currents of gratitude and hope for our lives
eddy and flow. In tandem we hold the trust we commit
to each other begets our vows to give of ourselves to each
other the best life possible for us to share.

Happy Valentine's Day, my love,
With all my love.

Night Flower

Tenderly sleep, my love, in my arms I open to you
like grateful soil receiving a summer rain.

Tenderly press your shoulders to my chest, your buttocks
to my groin, your thighs, calves and feet scissoring
with my own.

Tenderly breathe, your breath is relaxed, even, rhythmic,
a gentle warmth on my arm, sustenance for my soul.

Tenderly dream, my love, flights of joy for our spirits
entwined, we awaken refreshed, our roots watered.

With all my love.

Midday Note

Sweet baby, dance me slow and intimate, ambling
soft inside times of delicious pause, prolonged;
your warm lips pressed to mine, taking your leave,
again coming home – how was your day? better now?

With all my love,

My Rave Review

I need only think of you to remember how it feels
to be embraced without reservation.

Whenever the creative output of my artistic mind
comes back undervalued, making a life to house our love
gives me a purpose in faltering moments
when little else I do seems to matter.

Your laugh reminds me just what in our life holds the most
value.

Falling asleep in your arms, I know that tomorrow holds
promise.

With all my love,

Ministry

Sweet angel, you lift me up on the wings of your smile
and take me with you on your celestial flight as you
shout your joy to the heavens.

You envelope me with your love and whisper your peace
over my fear and self-doubt until my soul surrenders
to your belief in me. Then you take me gently to our bed,
and again bring me to rapture at the glory of your ministry
as the guardian angel of my life's delight.

Here's wishing you the happiest of holidays,
with all my love,

Held Securely in Your Arms

I relax; my time becomes easy.
 I experience what it means to love you forever
 as beginnings and endings disappear,
 and all that matters are your arms holding me
 close to your warmth.

We begin and end our days in each other's arms,
 and whenever we need, we seek that place of comfort
 and renewal.

Most of what we know of one another we've learned
 from touch.

You press intimate through openings, probe within places
 of me that I cannot see; you rub against my secrets
 and make them your own, bring me with you
 to where our knowledge of each other breaks into ecstasy.
 You place gently within me your love promises
 to open more each day.

Happy anniversary,
 with all my love,

My Music Man

Sing me sweet, my baby makes music on my flesh,
 pounds out the beat of his love; vibrates harmonics
 up and down my spine.

Sing me sweet, my baby carries me up scales and intervals,
then slides me down over his octaves, way low-down low,
to the bass of his jive.

Sing me sweet, my baby swings me, lays his lyrics all over
my body and soul, sets his vibrato inside my eyes.

Sing me sweet, my baby's music awakens me to my life
each day, over and over, holding the notes of his caresses,
the rhythm of his breath soft on my skin each night.

Sing me sweet, my baby shouts ecstatic trills, then sighs
the sigh of a man happy with life, secure in his love.

My baby holds me like an instrument he cherishes,
like a precious violin on which he bows his passion
as if intent on setting the strings afire.

My baby knows me, knows my melodies and my moods,
sings strong back-up to my reluctant solo, will improvise
a tune to lift me from my gloom.

Sing me sweet harmony in my ears whenever I hear
his name, a symphony of mysteries within the familiar
sound of his voice.

Sing me sweet, my baby loves me, loves to play his music
on my heart each day, and every day I gladly send it
right back at him.

With all my love — happy Valentine's Day.
Here's from me to you, and back, my love!

At Home

We have our home in each other, my love,
 we live in the space of us which you and I together are.

Have I told you enough how deeply secure I feel in your arms?

With all my love,

Your Gift

Your gift is that you make me simple:
 the weight of your thigh pressing on mine,
 our fingers entwined, your breath on my neck
 there are no more questions.

With all my love.

Nursing an Injury

My man got fired.
 A messed up, closeted queen
 couldn't have him, then
 didn't want him around

Accountability Award last year,
 then came the promotion,
 but my man failed to attend
 the queen's Christmas party,

Declined the queen's invitation
 to stay overnight without me.
Suddenly started getting
 bad reviews

My man got fired.
 Didn't shed a tear,
 felt nothing but relief,
 left and never looked back

Yes, my man got fired,
 but he's doing fine.
 I, on the other hand
 am plotting revenge

Vindication!

My love,
 as fastidious as you are
 about your appearance
 or the cleanliness
 of our home,
 so am I
 about your name.

As you have seen,
 if anyone soils it,
 I will scrub them away.

An evil, envious, closeted queen
 just got fired, and your dismissal
erased from the file.

With all my love,

Fifth Anniversary

Amid a hectic day
 I am removed
to a time and place for love
each time I hear your voice

I return from exasperation
over life's struggles
to joy and gratitude

_whenever I remember
that at the end of the day
the night is ours to share.

Your name holds for me
 all that I need to know
of how to live at peace
in a world of confusion.

Throughout the hours
 of doing our lives
I am sustained
by the sanctuary we create
whenever we touch.

Throughout the years
 of our changing bodies
 and circumstances,
 we are held steady
 by the love we hold ready
 to give to one another.

Happy Anniversary, my love
 with all my love,

Elemental

Your presence in my life is a precious, natural element.
 a vaporous proliferation of sustaining molecules in the air,
 a nutrient enriching the soil from which my thoughts grow
 the essential, animating vitality of refreshing waters,
 the burning soul of my desire to exist in a better state.

You inhabit my recollection, cognition, and anticipation.
 Your name and mine reside together in time, entwined
 both in our history and in our hopes, an entity
 without which we can no longer imagine ourselves
 except as a story already told, yet still in the telling.

Happy Valentine's Day, my love,
 with all my love.

Chapter 5 –
Celebrations

Stephen, my love,

You are the mysterious package I'm most anxious to unwrap this holiday season—your memories, stories, beliefs, all the pieces of your history that come together to make you the man I'm discovering: a man who delights in life and feels for others, who presents no pretense, who knows himself and is comfortable with that knowledge, who loves to play both naughty and nice, a man whose wild physical passion is born of a gentle, caring spirit.

Merry Christmas to you, Solstice to me, and a very Happy New Year to us both. Here's hoping we see many more together.

With all my love,

Gift Wrap

For the ribbon, let me use
  the waterfall of emotions I feel
  every time I look at your face.

Let me fashion a bow
 as complex and serene
 as your soul.

Let the pattern on the paper
 represent every act of kindness
 you've ever shown me.

Let this gift be one
 you never tire of receiving,
 and one you'll always return.

Merry Christmas, my love,
 With all my love.

Behind the Baubles

Whatever little things you receive
 bought or made for your delight,
 gussied up in colorful paper, wrapped
 in a velvet binding of ribbons,
 punctuated with an exclamatory bow
 as promising as a kiss blown
 from across a crowded room
 with a nod toward a private balcony

Whatever gifts I choose to bestow,
 accompanied by declarations of my love
 and appreciation for all the comfort and joy,
 the glad tidings you bring to me
 throughout the year as our lives,

our home, our trust entwine
with the kindness of the intimacies we share

These are but tokens of the greater joy
we know as we open our hearts and minds
to give and receive beyond ourselves,
from a deeper purpose, a universal reason
for celebrating this season of goodwill.

Merry Christmas, my love.
Here's wishing us another Happy New Year to share.

With all my love,

Our Weary World Rejoices

Even if the lights began to glitter a bit late this year,
with barely a week to cross the miles between,
envelopes still lay blank, awaiting addresses,
as the post office remained sold out of holiday stamps,
and the tree, which was lucky just to be lit,
had not a single gift beneath its boughs –

Even if the jobs we felt fortunate to still have
seemed enough for two or three to share,
and afforded no spare lunch hours during which,
say, a holiday poem for one's love might be written,
and even if our evenings were filled with everyday duties,
to the detriment of preparing for making merry

Nonetheless, my love, goodwill was not late to arrive.
We assisted each other in working through aches and pains,
we massaged scalps to relieve headaches,
took care to listen with sympathy,
reassured one another that with grace and gratitude
we would prevail by preparing concoctions of art and music
as tonic for frayed nerves.

Even in exhaustion—or especially in exhaustion
this gift of goodwill, the essence of this holiday, manifests.
Not in cards arriving on time or gifts wrapped in splendor,
nor in a home decked in fanciful array, sparkling clean,
nor even in the lines of this annual poem,
a tradition I cherish, though all these
be fun and satisfying signs of its presence –

Rather, the essence of this holiday is the comfort and joy
of knowing that to care for another expands the meaning
of life, that joy to the world makes requisite for its celebration
a wise concern for the wellbeing of others.

Merry Christmas, my love.
Here's wishing us a very Happy New Year to share,
I with you, and you with all my love.

Three Skin Tomes:

*(for Stephen, inspired by and in celebration of Barack
Obama's becoming the Democratic Party's presidential
candidate, June 4, 2008)*

I.   On the Eve

Every night you tug on me until my back skin
  nestles up close against your belly skin.
Then we switch, my convex belly pressed
into the concave curve of your lower spine.
Our fingers entwine to form two large fists,
  sprouting two thumbs and eight fingers, conjoining
  four arms into two coordinated limbs wrapped tight
around this comfortable, familiar night package
that soothes our thoughts of the day into shared sleep.

II.   One Entity, Under God

It's not often that I notice our skin anymore,
  how yours is milk-chocolate brown, mine a pinkish beige.
  Even that first evening we met, my attraction to you
had little to do with our contrasting levels of melanin.
Rather, it was the similarity of our smiles,
  our shared laughter, the sense of ease, of familiarity,
  of somehow having known you so long already.
It felt less like meeting than remembering,
a discovery of having already shared common space,
having already prepared room for you in my life,
knowing you would arrive.

III.   A Vote of Confidence

Today we are right next door
to having our first Black president
in this country where up until now
it hadn't seemed at all true
that any child could grow up
to move into the Oval Office.
No matter how often we heard that adage,
it mattered more that we'd never seen it practiced,
that it was a dream for some far distant morning.
Well today, at long last, comes that dream's awakening.

My love, lay down
this year with me

Around you, pull tight the memories; keep warm this dream
to which each morning we awaken, and again each night
take to sleep, to rest securely entwined in the arms
of our shared presence. Then again we awaken,
and we kiss, glad for the company of each other's spirit.

My love, lay down with me this year and again the next.
Take hold of my passion, offered freely, my hands
teasing around your own to let loose the groaning,
writhing ride of flesh upon flesh upon lips upon flesh.

My love, lay down with me to laugh this year,
to plan and worry and make do with our two lives,
a couple joined as together we arrange the space we inhabit
into our first home, which becomes the first story we tell.

Lay down with me, my love, to play, to rest,
  to sleep and rise again, to laugh and arrange,
  to speak and keep silent, to hold and release.
  Let us make of our lives together the center
  of all that we want for ourselves and each other;
  to see in each other that one by whom we know
  of all the lovely things in our life
  to love another as we love ourselves is the most dear.

Happy Anniversary, with all my love.

Designing Us

My love, sometimes our harmony
  must improvise to incorporate a sour note.
  Sometimes we bump heads in single-minded haste
  as we hurry each other along
  toward accomplishing a shared goal.

Sometimes we're a bit slow to yield creative control,
  to see our vision realigned so as to better
  suit form to function, to hear alternate rhythms
  opening new possibilities for our dance.

Without a doubt, we are both artists
  of undeniable genius in our designs
  for each other and our life together.
  But, we are not always without
  creative differences of opinion
  in the execution of this project called *us*.

Nonetheless, through fret and worry,
 and despite often resisting the obvious,
 somehow we always accomplish
 another day, another month, another year of patina,
 another layer of grace, a deeper respect
 for the creative process we share,
 for the living art we recognize
 expressed in each other.

Happy Valentine's Day, my love,
 With all my love,

Rapt in Conversation

So often in our conversations, my love,
 I feel you wrap your big, warm soul around me
 and sit back to listen as I snuggle close
 and confide in you my thoughts and speculations.
 Then you'll give me your take on the subject
 as I gladly give you that same attentive ear.

I am captivated by the broad intelligence of your soul
 and honored to be its beneficiary. You have
 extrasensory perception into the inner makings of people
 and the unlikely situations in which they find themselves.
 Yours is a wise intelligence.

You're not confounded by contradictions;
 you step back and look at them from a different angle.
 You see spectrums, not just this or that,
 but the this *and* that, and all the convolutions in between.

Yours is a gentle, accommodating truth,
more often a translucent glow that beckons us toward it
than a harsh beacon that sharply defines us in a moment.

You're like that with me. You don't judge me by my moments;
instead, you beckon me to be my overall best.
I cherish our conversation, stretching out now
over thirteen years, and still it often seems
like it's just beginning, that we're still getting acquainted
with whole areas of each other's lives and thoughts
we've yet to explore.

I hope this conversation, exchanged in words and silences,
in looks, gestures, embraces, in joint toil and labor,
in gifts and laughter—keeps going strong
for many, many more years and decades to come,
and which, for all we know, might last forever.

Happy Anniversary, my love,
With all my love,

To Know Deep Satisfaction

My love, I am not complacent in our love,
rather, each year I am more deeply satisfied
to see us meet the only standard by which
I measure the quality of our lives together:
that we be honest with ourselves and each other
in our first desire to share the best life possible
for each of us to live.

Yours is the only body I can hold at night
and know there is always a purpose for the day.
Only the touch of your skin brings serenity to my sleep,
promises refuge no matter what new challenges
might rise with the sun. Only the warm wafting of your breath
into the shared air of our night brings reverie to my dreams.

Happy Anniversary, my love,
With all my love,

A Cozy, Practical Holiday

My thoughts about our holiday celebration this year
are somewhat scattered, a bit out of focus.
The whirl is still distant, I'm not yet caught up in its winds.
This year I feel like being ordinary, relaxed, and a little lazy.
I'm happy to pour us a bit of wine, sit back, enjoy
each other's company.

No need to perform feats of high festivity,
wrap ourselves in ribbons and cook a twelve-day feast.
We can do very well with just a few treats, the great luxury
of taking the time to enjoy them together.

My greatest delight of the holiday season is always
simply to share this celebration of goodwill with you.
So for this holiday, I'd like to wrap up a bit of peace and quiet,
to share a string of evenings to work on our music and art,
to watch a movie, converse at our leisure, to take a sip
of holiday cheer amid simple decorations, with deep,

complex appreciation for one another and this world
we are blessed to share.

Merry Christmas and Happy New Year, my love,
With all my love,

Seventh Anniversary – *Belief*

The years having passed
become our future,
bode well for our tomorrows
and our history beyond.

You decipher my eyes,
parse the resonance of my speech,
apprehend the precise meaning
of each hug, recognize
the matrix of each kiss.

You make me realize
that being known so intimately
is a privilege,
a rare opportunity
as is also your invitation
for me to know inside you.

You teach me to live each day
in anticipation of its memory.

Happy Anniversary, my love,
with all my love.

Glad Tidings

My love, come celebrate
love suffuses this day within us
grows an urge to embrace
with joy we reach out to others
likewise touch us with benevolence.

Celebrate, my love, the holiday lights
entice us to laugh wise laughter
fills the emptiness of want
with charity and cheer for all
warms the cold night.

Let us celebrate each candle beckons
peace is born of justice
is born of goodwill
is proclaimed this day
is still possible.

With ornament and glitter,
with gold, frankincense, and myrrh,
with new ritual and old tradition,
we assert hope renews courage
overcomes suspicion and fear.

My love, celebrate our tenderness
brings harmony to our world
extends beyond us await people
of kindred desires join in this season
to compel the dream forward.

Wishing you all the happiness
 of this joyous holiday,
 with all my love.

Christmas Joy

Sweet snuggle, my love
 comes another season of festivities,
 another celebration of awakening light
 coming to darkened earth.

A story of infinite joy, eternal, timeless,
 forever and always the source
 from which we birth new life.
 The story of another generation,
 of hope for humanity,
 of a new face among us
 turning to grow toward the sun.

Merry Christmas, my love.
 May we celebrate many another season
 of goodwill in the warmth of each other's arms,
 with all my love.

The Lover's Prayer

Let me saturate my mind
  with gratitude
  for the joy he brings to my life,
  with appreciation
  for the music that flows from his soul,
  with love
  for all the humanity I see in his face.

Let me hallow the fact of us
  with honor
  for those who taught us how to love,
  with remembrance
  of the pain from which love delivers us,
  with reverence
  for the mystery we now hold between us.

Let me inform my every exchange
  with kindness
  akin to the impulse he excites in me,
  with charity
  in my perception of the other's purpose,
  with knowledge
  that one can truly desire another's happiness.

For our love,
  with all my love.

Love Unlimited

How many different words
  can say *I love you*?

How many different smiles
  say *I love you too*?

How many lives
  can love awaken?

How many dreams
  can love realize?

It's unlimited.
  Love is unlimited.

How much beauty
  can grow in a spirit?

How much truth
  remains to be known?

How many times
  can a soul feel joyful?

How many days
  begin with sunrise?

It's unlimited.
  Love is unlimited.

How much good
  can come from kindness?

How much peace
  does our world need now?

How much love
  can we give to one another?

How much light
  do you bring into my life?

It's unlimited.
  Our love is unlimited.

Celebration

In this season of gifts,
  what better present to open
  than my eyes each morning
  to the sight of you, content?

In this season of ribbons,
  what wrapping more splendid
  than your honesty
  when you say that you love me?

In this season of fantasy and myth,
  what tale better to weave
  than the truth of our lives entwined?

In this season of candles,
  how better to celebrate light
  than to hold you in my thoughts?

In this season of home and family,
  where better to find security
  than in making our history?

Wishing you the happiest of holidays,
  with all my love.

My love, let me wrap you in words this winter

Let me speak memory and hope
  and laughter and love.
  Let me speak of your smiles,
  of the smirk you wear
  that tells me when you're going to be naughty,
  or that you know I know you told me so.

Let me speak of your face ignited with delight
  at a gift you didn't know I knew you wanted,
  or of the sleepy little smile each morning
  when, eyes barely open, you stick out your lips
  for a kiss.

Let me wrap my words around you
  to tell you of my happiness
  that the joy you brought me at this time last year
  has grown cozy and made itself at home,

that the jewelry box with my apartment's keys
  has proven as much a gift to myself
  as it was an expression of my faith in you,

that to trust and love another once again
is a gift beyond words
a settled, joyful, silent knowing
that I am as much to you
as you are to me
loved beyond words.

With all my love.

Chapter 6 – Defining Our Destiny

In Our Utopia

Let us live together in a place of possible dreams,
 where you make your music as I write and make my art,
 where we have time and energy to tend to our bodies,
 where our only stress is our internal desire to create.

Let us sleep together at night wrapped
 in the beautiful exhaustion
 of having poured out our souls, then awaken refreshed
 to another day full of promise.

Let our concerns be not only for our own ability to cope,
 but also for our ability to better the lives
 of those with whom we share our world.

Let us live so that the marks we leave behind us
 will lead others to discover their own best lives.

With all my love,

Love, With Wings

Thoughts of you come as updraft winds
that lift my mind above daily aggravations and concerns,
giving aerial perspective to flattened worries
on the landscape below.

You fly me free to a state of gratitude
for a life already blessed with love,
free to anticipate soaring into our future,
held aloft on the wings of ultimate trust.

I hope that in return I might likewise
give wing to what you imagine is possible for yourself,
hold you up with accolades for the honest and pure voice
you give to the music you create, for the impeccable style
with which you present yourself to the world;
hold you up with love for the kindness,
the joy and uplift of your spirit, for
the appreciative audience you so generously give
to others, for the vigilant and faithful concern
you always maintain for my well-being.

I hope that I uplift you with hope for a future
"moving on up" not just in age, but in satisfaction
knowing you have lived your life well
and that you are deeply loved.

I hope that I give you the freedom to dream
of flying to whatever heights you wish to attain,
confident of your own abilities,
confident of my appreciation and support,

confident that you fly accompanied by my prayers
for your happiness, your well-being,
and your safe return to my embrace.

Happy Birthday, my love, and happy flights,
With all my love,

With These Rings We Wear

We celebrate another year constant,
 knowing without need to ask each other why.

I know you know how every time I think of you
 I still feel that warm, sinking, tender sensation
 in my chest and throat,
 how readily, in the midst of a working day,
 the muscle memory of my arms recalls our embrace,
 how often my body yearns to touch your fire,
 how deliciously ripe and many years strong
 is my desire for you.

Within our daily music we live
 a complex weave of melodic lines
 always fresh with infinite variations
 overlapping to fill our home with harmonies,
 quiet meditations, brassy declarations,
 celebratory rumbas, bawdy burlesques,
 shout-and-praise gospel, stylish jazz,
 house beats that catch a groove and make a body move,
 soothing lullabies for lovers entangled fast asleep
 in a bed made up of hopes and memories.

We celebrate another year constant,
　knowing our desire is to make of our home
　a place of refuge and regeneration,
　the bosom of our life together,

To make of ourselves partners worthy of each other's trust,
　each the one to whom the other would give his voice
　were he unable to speak,

To make of our life together one
　we would gladly and without hesitation choose again,
　one we are proud to signify
　with unending circles of solid gold.

Happy Anniversary, my love,
　With all my love,

My 'Stand By Me' Man

Your eyes, steady, patient, honest,
　relieve my mind of doubts and troubles,
　replacing concerns with trust in our future.

Your embrace, strong and committed,
　reminds my soul that we are secure
　in our destiny, secure in our love,
　able to endure.

Your body, contoured with mine in our bed,
　reawakens my desire to live life
　in joy and pleasure.

Your name, spoken with mine,
 is all I need to know
 that my life has a cherished purpose
 beyond myself.

Happy Valentine's Day, my love,
 With all my love,

Charles, My Love, Stephen

The thought of you excites in me
 a profound sense of gratitude,
 one I know will abide and grow
 for so long as I know my own name
 and maybe well beyond.

I delight that we are destined
 to be remembered together,
 that our lives cannot be told complete
 without naming us both.

For fourteen years
 I have welcomed you into my story
 and gladly stepped into your own.
 We have become words spoken together,
 two personalities conveyed in one breath.
 Our names have joined to tell the story
 we have been blessed to share.

We are two and one in the eyes
 of all that is sacred and true,
 Mr. & Mr. Hughes-Luing.

Happy Anniversary, my love,
 With all my love,

Simply Love

My love, we experience our love
 as a smooth, beautiful simplicity
 because we appreciate and accommodate
 the complexities of each other and of ourselves.

In the security of our each having met with death
 and stepped beyond evaporating illusions
 to reach the place where the spiritual
 is physical is intellectual is emotional is our reality,
 where the invisible core of ourselves is solid,
 we have learned to become real to ourselves,
 and with each other.

We have learned to connect at a place
 where connection is not so much understanding
 as incorporation, where we embrace mystery.

You are as familiar and mysterious to me
 as I am to myself, and as connected.

I am to you as you are to me
 as we are to our world, married.

Happy Valentine's Day, my love,
 With all my love,

If Only an Audience of One

My love, my fellow artist,
 my singer of your soul's pure voice,

we've both put our art out in public,
 and so far the public hasn't given it much notice.

I think we need not despair;
 perhaps it's better that we live, love,
 and express our creativity in anonymity,
 that we keep each other and our art
 to ourselves and a select few.

Shakespeare tells us:
 "Love all, trust a few, and hurt none."
 So maybe while we can love all
 and hurt none with our art,
 we're better off entrusting it
 only to those who seek it out.

Do we know what creatures we might become with fame?
 How fortune could alter the mindful balance
 within the walls of the home in which we live?
 Do we trust ourselves to find out?

With recognition come expectations,
 perhaps limitations.

We are never so free as we are when unobserved,
able to express ourselves
with only our imaginations to advise us.

A persona, a press agent, public relations
all might exhaust,
might undermine our private lives,
our intimate relations.

Or perhaps we might indeed rise to the challenge,
prove ourselves capable of success with success.

Perhaps we need to embrace ourselves either way,
whether we are seen and heard by a few or by many,
care not if praised for red one day
and for blue the next.

Perhaps we need only know
that whatever we do with our art,
we will be loved by each other
for our effort and imagination,
for the quality of life our art enables us to create.

Happy Valentine's Day, my love,
You are the music of my life,
With all my love.

Our Mutual Fund

My love, ours is a simple life.

We work our jobs, maintain our home,
 find a little time for our art and music,
 and in all things seek to nurture each other.

We sleep soundly at night, rise early,
 and appreciate our every day together.
 This has been our rhythm for eleven years now,
 and I am happy for it.

Ours is not a life of extravagant means,
 but in terms of what in life has true value,
 we are abundantly rich.

No gemstone shines more precious to me
 than the tone in your voice when you call me your man.
 No security is greater than the certainty of your love.
 No return more rewarding
 than walking through the door of our home.

Our every embrace is a dividend paid
 on years of well-invested trust.
 Our every conversation is compounded interest
 in one another's well-being.

Even your patient silence as you wait for storms to pass
 is rich in nurture,
 a balm to every injury my artistic ego endures

when hours of drawing end in scraps of paper,
or an entire meal is marred by a less-than-perfect dish.

We bank away care given and care received
on a ledger that always balances,
a ledger which counts partnership as principal.

You are for me, as I am for you,
the joint custodian of each day's potential for joy.

And at night, when we curl up together,
arranging the covers so you are cocooned
and I am half exposed,
we find mutual comfort knowing
we best secure our shared assets
by accommodating the needs and nurturing the interests
of each particular party
to this long-term growth account.

Happy 11th Anniversary, my love,
With all my love.

Vows

I.

Because of you,
beyond me is *us*.

All that I desire for myself
I now desire for us.

For me to believe something is good for me,
 I must believe it is good for us.

To be myself is now
 to be part of a greater whole.

I give what I am to us,
 and become more.

II.

Wherever you are,
 I am aware of your presence.

Yours is the first name I know
 beyond my own.

For others to know
 the full meaning of my name,
 they must know yours.

You alone may know my name
 as intimately
 as you know your own.

III.

Within my embrace there is room
 for your every mood, every delight or pain,
 each joy you experience,
 each lesson you learn.

There is room for every question you ask,
 every answer you find.
 For every declaration of your life,

there is room for you to be yourself
within my embrace.

IV.

Whenever we touch,
 my spirit entwines with yours
 in answer to our first desire
 for warmth, comfort, safety,

A place to call home,
 a place to which we return
 after each expedition,

A place at ease,
 where body and soul regenerate,
 a place of sanctity,
 where we are secure
 in the exposure of our most intimate selves
 to one another.

Happy Valentine's, my love,
 With all my love,

Marriage Proposal

My love, will you give me your name
 and accept from me my own?

I want to be an honest man
 and declare to the scribes
 that the life I have chosen is not singular,
 it is entwined

so that any decision I make affects you,
and any choice you make
is one with which I, too, am willing to live.

If to be moral we must be trustworthy
with ourselves, each other, and our world,
then you are the first test beyond myself
of how truthful a person I can be.

If God is love,
and love sets us free
to connect with others beyond ourselves,
then every day you are my best chance
to share in the liberation of God's love.

If ever I lose my capacity to decide, then
from all the looks we have exchanged,
from words, silences, and sighs,
from all you have seen
of the workings of my body and mind,
I want you to answer on my behalf
the questions we could not foresee.

When future genealogies are written,
I want your name to be joined with mine
to speak of the place we have created
from the histories we have combined
to make of our life together
a mark of honor befitting both
our predecessors and our heirs.

My love, will you combine with me
the names we bring to each other?
Will you marry me?

Chapter 7 – *Response*
For My Husband

Wings of Love
by Charles Stephen Hughes

As we both rush off to work each day, tending to our tasks, then come home sometimes too tired to make it to a workout at the gym, yet you still prepare the most amazing dinners, I marvel at your commitment, which never wavers.

At night, as we lay down to sleep, your loving arms cradle me. I move in closer, and you pull me tighter into your embrace. You gently kiss the back of my neck, and together we soothe the chaos of our day. Wrapped in these wings of love, I know God smiles down upon us, pleased.

When you sit at the computer, working out our expenses, I sometimes catch the look of concern on your face. I know you worry about our financial stability, as I do too. With the world in crisis, so many people each day wonder how they will manage. Yet I thank God that we are both still blessed with jobs and security. I believe with all my heart that our love, and God's wings of love, will always protect us through the days and years ahead.

Even the smallest things – when you brush your teeth and make that cute monkey face, saying, "I'm letting my tooths air out", or when you wrestle with whether your beautiful artwork is "good enough," or when you hear a song you love and dance sexy to the beat – each of these moments makes me fall more in love with you every day.

So here's to our future, our lives, our health, our finances. May our wings always grow together, entwined for eternity, guided by God's gift of love to grow old and wise.

CSH

Stephen with his mom, Liz, and me at our wedding in San Francisco's City Hall

Postscript

Vows Exchanged – July 23, 2013

(Prior to our official wedding ceremony in San Francisco's City Hall that day, each stanza repeated, one to the other)

Devotion

Know that my life is devoted to looking out for your best interests, that I will treat your needs and desires as equal to my own, that I will not consider anything good for me if it is not good for us and the life we share. And know that I am secure in the knowledge that the same is true for you with respect to me. Our interactions with others will always be conducted so as to maintain and strengthen the trust we have in each other.

Fidelity

You are the first person with whom I will share a joy or a sorrow, a fear or a conviction. You are the first to read the story of me as it is written each day, the only person with rights to access all the words as they are laid down—unedited and uncensored—the one I most trust to know, understand, and protect the truth of who I am. And I want you to know, without question, that you may rely on me to be that same person for you. To be true to myself, I must know, understand, and protect the truth of who you are.

Honor

I gladly make known to the world that you are the keeper of the artifacts of my life, an equal partner in the business of the life we share, an equal voice in how we make and manage our home and all that we own in common. I gladly enter into the annals by which our society is ordered the declaration that you are the person whom I trust to make my decisions and handle my affairs if I am unable to do so for myself, that you are the person to whom I give control even of my body if I am unable to manage it for myself, and that you are the person I entrust with the closure of my life should you outlive me.

Joy

In as many ways as I am able, I will bring you pleasure and delight. I will seek to nurture and enliven your spirit, to celebrate and appreciate your self-expression. I will meet your creativity with my own so that together we may discover new ways to explore and understand our connection with Creation and the Creator, the many and one whose soul we share, in whose expression and endurance we participate with our every breath.

Perpetuity

We are the known in the unknown. Together we will share unseen blessings, and together we will face unforeseen challenges. Together we reach beyond ourselves to embrace our shared destiny, whatever it may be. For better or worse, for richer or poorer, in sickness and in health, come what may we are now joined in history, even should death do us part.

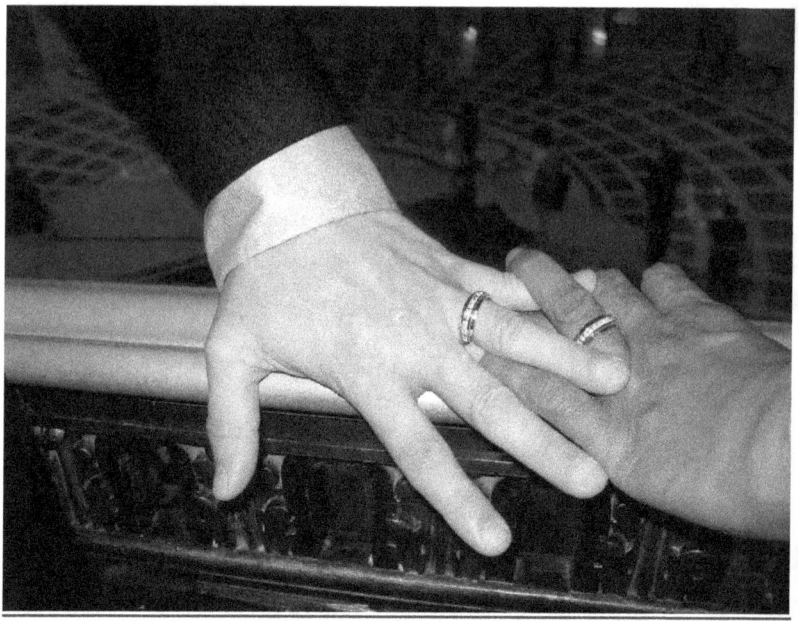

Book 4:
Aftermath

Foreword

This is not about anything real, just things I don't remember. Memories for which I've saved pieces but no longer recall the patterns for how they fit together.

Memories reach for what happened, grasp bits and pieces of the past, pull portions into the present, and in that process inevitably scrape loose fragments that fall away into oblivion.

Then words fill in those scrapes. But the pictures with which we are left are truer to who we are now than to who we were then. I never see the same face in my mirror.

Chapter 1 –
The Aftermath Begins

For most of my adult life I was Philip and _____. In that blank are the four names accompanying my own on a headstone in a cemetery now two days by express train away. Each name is followed by beginning and end dates. The end date for mine, though it has felt finished more than once, remains uncarved.

The first died instantly in a car crash. For the other three, I was bedside at their deaths. I provided care throughout their decline and final illness, then planned their funerals and closed their affairs. I learned that one can be given no more precious, more intimate a gift than to be allowed to help someone die well.

Each of the four has a permanent place in my life. But if you ask me where, I cannot recall their precise locations. I try to remember their faces apart from my recollection of fading photographs I no longer possess, try to recall things we did together apart from what I once wrote down. I cannot. I get lost trying to find them. Curtains have been drawn to close out the piercing light of any well-articulated memory. My eyes have developed photophobia. I must wear dark glasses.

writing only thoughts
my memory holds outlines
leaves blank my insides

I write now to find a way home, to complete that headstone. The story deserves an ending, though I have little to remind me how it got here. All I have are words written before memory lost its hold on detail.

dry memories, words
letters in groups, forming lines
no colors or smell

My question is how to lay these lives to rest. How to allow my mind to rest with them. How not to confuse *lay* with *lie*.

how do I let go
my memories are empty
no hold to release

I would be hard-pressed to embellish these bare notes with colors, odors, emotions, names, causes, principles, or lessons.

lust | death | words engage
writers give readers feelings
I cannot bring back

What we know is that the end did not come on April Fool's Day 2018, which was also Easter Sunday that year, the day I became homeless.

a hairbrush, grooming
never using a mirror
my face forgotten

What I have instead are dates, fixed by calendars, stabilizing reference points. I can at least note when my last Christmas occurred.

December 2012

Instead of two tickets for our first vacation to Key West, we opted for three tickets to return to San Francisco, having so enjoyed our first visit. His mother had never been there, though she'd loved hearing our stories.

She'd just retired after decades driving a CTA bus in Chicago. She had only flown once, with two co-workers, to vacation in Aruba.

She could strike up conversation with anyone, though you never knew what she might tell a stranger.

That was Mom. More like a young aunt or older sister: there for fun, but she always got to work, too.

She gave money to her mother, grandmother, and aunt to help raise her kids. Responsible in her way. Reliable. A mooch if you let her, but never sore if you didn't.

She'd lost one son, Eric, gunned down at his father's home on the South Side one Labor Day while she was visiting us.

Taking Lake Shore Drive, our cabbie prayed aloud. On arrival she was ushered into the family room to hear the news.

Now, a decade later, for Christmas we surprised her with a trip back with us to San Francisco.

2013

He began eating less, losing weight. His doctor had advised losing twenty pounds. He mentioned a minor ache in his side, thought he was using too much weight at the gym.

We were planning to marry soon in Illinois. The legislature was expected to approve same-sex marriage that spring, but delayed until fall. Meanwhile, in June, Proposition 8 in California fell.

We reserved a spot at San Francisco City Hall for our wedding that July. His mother was delighted to be our witness.

That week, his side ached enough that he called his doctor. Suspected gallbladder. Scheduled an ultrasound. Instead:

A large tumor. Two. More. A web of tumors. Liver, lungs. Stage four. Silent until they pressed outward. No nerves in the liver itself.

Brave Love

"Am I going to die?"

Just he and I. Eye to eye. Unblinking. The plaintive question. I was the only one he would ask. That memory, that trust, is among the most intimate, precious gifts I have ever received. I answered as honestly as I could, that it was a possibility which we were doing everything we could to prevent from happening.

November 15, 2013

The day after our fifteenth anniversary. Three days before his fiftieth birthday. He died in our home, on our bed, me at his side, holding him. His mom and siblings waited in the dining room for word from the hospice nurse.

Afterward

I tried to return to work in December, but felt I was failing. In January I offered my resignation; it was declined. Instead, an outpatient day hospital was recommended for February.

I returned in March. In April, stroke-like symptoms landed me in the ER. The neurologist suspected a medication reaction. Symptoms resolved in weeks.

In June, two sudden vacancies meant I was covering specialized duties which no one else understood. I worked 12–16 hour days, seven days a week, often pulling all-nighters. I fell behind. My supervisor urged "better concentration." I promised more. Became disoriented. Got lost while walking among buildings I'd walked for decades.

That November, on what would have been our sixteenth anniversary, I took our wedding vows in a clear sleeve to Hollywood Beach. In icy wind and rain, waves crashing above my head, I shouted our vows into the storm.

When I turned back, a lifeguard in orange and yellow stood silently near the lighthouse. We nodded. Perhaps I had created a memorable story for us both.

After struggling with ongoing, overwhelming confusion, in November of 2014, I gave notice at work. HR suggested retirement instead, the following March, when I would be eligible.

In March, 2015 after working for thirty years at the institution, I retired. In June I purchased an idyllic, two-bedroom, live-in artist's studio along a salmon stream in southern Oregon for my retirement. In 2017, from April to July, I experienced a series of debilitating strokes, rendering me unable to maintain my home, which I sold to finance my stay at an assisted care complex. Lacking adequate social services to help me file for disability properly, my application was denied, and my funds ran out after the payment of my March, 2018 rent. In despair, overwhelmed with grief, and depleted of funds, I left behind everything I owned and took a bus toward the Oregon Coast, where I intended to drown myself.

It didn't work, and I ended up instead staying at a homeless shelter in Eugene, Oregon from April 2018 through May 2019, then traveled, made various temporary arrangements, and finally found my way to housing and medical care in

Albuquerque, New Mexico, where I secured housing, transitional at first, then longer term.

In the dry, even climate, my debilitating arthritic inflammation diminished as my neurological recovery progressed.

Able to type on a keyboard, focus my mind to write.

2020

By May I was once again able to hold a paintbrush steady enough to resume easel painting for the first time since 2013. I'd stopped after Stephen's death.

At the OffCenter Community Arts Program's weekly writing group, I wrote:

Make Your Own Magic

My easel transports me
 on a magic carpet ride.
 I lift my paintbrush,
 wave it like a magic wand.
 Constraints evaporate.

Unfettered, I exalt,
 I rage, I flow.

Chapter 2 – *Finding Refuge in Writing:*

Trauma-Informed Poetry

<u>Detritus</u>

Salvaged Bits and Pieces of Poetry
Written During a Year in Residence at a Homeless Shelter
(Where My Daily Chore Was to Drive the Trash Truck)

Chalk Street Figure

In an emotional state of chalk
Firm, soft, powdery dust, messy
Of some use for communication
Nothing enduring, meant to be erased.

Self-Portrait, Redesigned, Resigned

I have died several times already, in other lives.

Now I am a lone, silvered, not-yet-mangy bison
  standing apart, watching, unblinking,
  awaiting the whiff of dank fur, putrid breath,
  jagged pain ripping through my neck signaling
  the arrival of wolves, coyote, cougar, bear
  whatever comes bringing the final takedown
  to release, to feed the time
  accumulated in my remaining blood
  back into the always hungry, regifting earth
  from which another life might grow.

To Be Filed Under

Things too big to be seen:

Silent, unmoving, unspoken pains,
  their presence only hinted at,
  Fleeting, ghostly grimaces
  twitching across otherwise expressionless faces.

Faces providing secret harbor,
  holding agony under passive cover,
  compressing pain into interior masses.

Desiccated, solid, fragile, like chalk
  prone to crumble, dissolve, leave smudges,
  marks easy to wipe away.

What Comfort

I sit encased in painted cement block walls,
 in colors meant to quiet
 butter, Dijon mustard,
 German Chocolate Cake brown on the doors.
 All are battered and scuffed,
 the floor tiles likewise,
 ceilings off-white, lit by searchlight fluorescents.

I sit here amidst a gathering of anxieties,
 garbed in exotic costumes of chance and choice,
 co-mingled in our clothes as in our life stories,
 impossible now to parse out, pointless anyway.

Various infestations on, under, inside various skins
 reside alongside kindness, yearning, jokes, laughter, fear,
 wonderings of what happened, and what yet might.

So human. So many humans. All so very different
 slipped off the edges of so many worlds,
 swept together in this room of battered colors
 meant to soothe. Wondering what, if anything.

Worth a try? Get back in the game
 and again be gamed by those

 writing un-leveling rules to their own advantage,
 dismissing our talents unless they translate
 cheaply, easily, into capital gains.

Relegating unrealized talent,
human resources in business terms,
to sit in a room of cement blocks,
garbed by chance and choice, as are they,
seeking to tune out worries
with TV and silent stares.

But a Song

Loss liberates.
I am all done doing
everything I needed to do in this life.

All done and gone, with nothing left to lose.
Janis, me, and Bobby McGee
know freedom.

No need any more to claim success
by my own measure or anyone else's,
free to follow whimsy, play with wishes.

I think I'd like to do something very kind
without knowing I had.
Invisibly, drifting.

Now in August 2018

Five years since. Two emotions.

Between them: featureless stretches,
 bland, intellectualized space, flat horizons.

My mind understands, recognizes, appreciates.
 Sees generosity, knows with certainty
 unfelt in my heart
 how this sort of thing brings good to life,
 benefits us all, like art,
 which I also once felt.

I express gratitude, give sincere if dry thanks.
 Mostly I feel anger
 as annoyance, irritation, discomfiture
 a ripple to let pass, not worth the trouble.

Nobody died just now, did they?
 Most violations fail to rise to that level.

And then, a peculiar sense without a word
 stoic, perhaps, but not emotion.
 More like intuition lurking,
 knowing without knowing how
 I am not allowing myself to cry.

After all, somebody did die, didn't they?
 Somebody, and somebody, and somebody, and
 yet again, somebody. And many others, also close.

Now, everything lost, all mementos of loss lost.
 Yet nothing feels gone or present,
  just space recollected blankly,
   with not even an empty feeling.

Waking, 5:30 a.m.

Fragments. Dark blocks. Edges of light.
 Sharp, elongated, triangular points, spears.

Falling apart, down through empty space,
 no air to breathe between the shrapnel.
  Silent motion, downward disintegration.

Becoming the world embedded in my mind,
 a world through which I pass every mourning.

Recollections

I cannot report what I cannot recall.
 I dare not measure the size of the holes
  suggesting what might be gone.

Mother, father, siblings, cousins, childhood friends.
 Playgrounds.

Ben in '74, funeral on my seventeenth birthday.
 I was a pallbearer. Tears shamed, buried.

Dennis in '84, banishment as protection.
 In '90, Dennis again, past love carried forward:
 caregiver, executor, friend delivering his eulogy.

Jeff in '94, twelve years, four of them in decline.
 Ashes scattered on the Oregon coast in '98.

By 2009, the last funeral before my own:
 twelve couples once woven into a safety net,
 now also gone, mostly as cremated remains.

Stephen in 2013, the one too many.
 Dying the day after our fifteenth anniversary.

2015: inflammation.
 2017: strokes.
 2018: loss of everything, forty years
 of art and memorabilia, gone in a truck.
 Two plastic bags, unhoused on Easter Sunday.

I fled to the Oregon coast,
 planned to wade west, offshore toward China.
 Instead, I landed in a homeless shelter.

Siblings expressed shock, sorrow, offers to help.
 But none really could. Silence mostly.
 Parents said they prayed I would "get right with God."

Too much to tell. I had not expected
 ever to see anyone again.

Dust in the Wind

Wind comes and goes,
 stirring up dust, sometimes more.

Eventually, dust settles
 along with everything else.
 Things change. Go on.

Some feelings fleet like the wind
 coming and going, moving things
 which then settle, changed a bit,
 or quite a bit.

Other times emotions come,
 but we catch and hold them.
 Instead of moving on,
 they burrow,
 sometimes so deeply
 they cannot leave
 until dug out, set loose,
 until allowed to stir our dust
 along with our lives.

Subjective Ease

What we see as flowing
 is to the stream a struggle
 against soil, sand, pebbles, rocks,
 huge boulders to reach the sea.

Only to be carried back again
 by clouds, set down, to repeat
 the downhill battle.

Evolution Redux

Sleep is the ocean
 from which our thoughts crawl
 each morning into light.

Each evening, they return,
 walk the shore,
 wade in, testing undertow.

One night, wading deeper, they
 will not return. Perhaps, if gifted peace,
 will not even try.

Yea, Though I, Through
the Valley

Dry walking. Dust walking.
 Eyes closed, or slits glancing
 not for direction, but to avoid.

No desire for contact.
 Neither to collide nor play.

Constant veiled observation.
 Occasional perceptions.
 Rarely shared.

A loner passing through
his own desert of choices.

Daybreak

Sunlight looks like sunlight,
the same as it did.

I hold up a prism. Light divides
into a new spectrum.

I don't know where to look.
Don't know how hope, or joy,
or even the desire for them
might appear in this new light.

Perhaps I will go back inside to look.

The Fire Poem (First Season)

We are surrounded by fire.

From every direction
comes the odor of living things
going up in smoke.

We remind ourselves:
the acrid odor
could be ourselves burning,
the smell of life
regenerating,

wiping clean the slate
for the next generation
to start anew
with dreams as big as ours.

Life comes from life
passing.

Fires Transforming
(Second Season)

What's useful now: my life lived
as abstract feelings. A country burns,
a countryside also, both in flames.

Fire is life giving way to life
comes from life passing
into indigenous dirt, melding soil
with familial bonds, ancestral wisdom,
reverence deep within boulders,
sand, wind, streams
fire burning us all down to the ground.

To bare roots bearing restoration,
health, nurture, opening earth
to seeds of change. We need not let go.
Ashes will fall through our fingers,
our fingers' ashes also

impossible to grasp. Memories,
true and false simultaneously,

blown further away into a time when.
Is anything saved, saved?

We are, at best, of use temporarily,
 tending restorative roots
 growing within our own soil.
 And always, again, the coming fire
 will reignite, consume, renew.

Living the Dreamy Life

Something I dreamt last night made sense.
 I don't remember the dream, or dreams,
 any dream or the thing in it that made sense.

It may not have made sense.
 I may have dreamt it did.

I'm describing how I experience life now,
 if that now makes sense.

Did it ever?
 I live in dreams I can't recall.

Sweeping Up Dust

Everything becomes dust eventually,
 blows away, even our own
 constantly adrift, traveling
 over continents, seas.

Rendering sunsets with colors to inspire
others to feel awe, others who may
or may not remember us,
who may or may not talk about us much,
if at all.

But they will watch sunsets.
They will feel our fading fire,
and connect.

Proceed with Caution

Dark mood, dull patch of pavement,
stressed underneath, surface smooth.
Appears unbroken, useful,
easy to walk over

without tripping, stubbing toes,
without noticing, thinking anything of it.
Doesn't take much effort,
helps to get you there.

No promises for the way back,
should you return
or wish to.
I could easily be gone.

Our Enlightened Self
in Monochrome

I imagine an ashen gray lump of clay,
 smoothed, rounded, moist,
 turned in on itself in a fetal shape,
 an ashen gray bean abiding its time
 in an ashen gray, featureless landscape.

Little distinguishes it from its world
 save that I know it's there,
 slowly dehydrating, drying, fissuring,
 cracking, crumbling, falling apart,
 turning to rubble, then dust
 in ashen gray air.

At this point in my unintentional meditation
 I felt perfectly at peace,
 fell into deep, restful, blank sleep.

Like so many others,
 I could write an entire book
 about how nothing in this book means anything
 how even existential angst
 has lost its significance.

It doesn't mean much anymore.
 Not like it used to not.

No Hand-Me-Down Help

One cannot see exquisite beauty
 within a pile of festering pain
 by looking down on it from above.

But eye to eye, in pain simply met
 on its own level, we may glimpse beauty
 beneath its veil.

Nor from within pain's pile
 can we see beauty in those
 who bend over us,
 handing down help.

Gratitude is best felt mutually,
 reciprocity shared among equals,
 each both giving and taking,
 all benefiting.

We are none of us beyond help,
 none beyond the ability to help.
 We are all of us, all
 and all that any of us has to go on.

Recurrent Daze

Each day, a perfectly fine, doable chore,
 not much of a worry. Accomplished, gotten through.

I sleep with no sense of satisfaction,
 nor dread for tomorrow.
 No sense of beyond.

What I need is a padded cell,
 walls, floor, ceiling
 totally dark, soundproof.

There, I could weep, wail, scream,
 beat the floor, the walls,
 throw myself around and around until
 I am either dead or alive, released
 from this nonbeing,

this disconnection,
 my brain overfilled, ideas, perceptions
 none of them exciting passion, feeling.

I Am What I Hear

I am my thought plucking
 the string of nothing,
 making a sound
 that does not yet exist.

Small Craft Warning

I have no home in my brain.
 No mooring, no safe harbor.
 I am out to sea permanently.

No longer bothering to seal leaks,
  content to bail.

Thinking Inside the Box

I turn as if weightless
  within a cube, suspended
  by equal gravitational pulls
  from each of its six walls,
  as I try to learn my identity
  without external clues.

Beyond one wall: my past.
  Beyond its opposite: my future
  neither yet, or still, exists.

On either side: this unknown life
  I now live, unaware.

Above lies hope.
  Below lies despair.
  Or perhaps the reverse.
  I cannot yet tell.

All walls translucent,
  dim light glowing through
  similar colors, intensities.

Once I see myself clearly,
  I expect these walls will dissolve.

I will see where I am,
recognize who I am.
Finally I'll be why I am
being, simply to be
and then be still,
leaving no unsettled spirits behind.

Banquet

Each lovely memory becomes a ripping loose,
tearing tendons, blood vessels
a presence once in living color evaporating,
perspiring through my pores.

The sound of each forever-love aspirating,
passing over my lips
a pale spirit swallowed as it rises, freed of me
by that dark, relentlessly famished translucence:
death.

It leaves me few crumbs to savor.
Which I do.

Veiled

Not so much lost in a fog
as escaped into several.

Living forgotten memories,
I am not so much lost

as self-forgotten,
an occult presence
living among the not-yet-lost.

No Matter

I exist in the not-present:
  not here, not now, not there, not then.

Time's bleak flow erodes, obliterates
  recognizable features,
  exposing an anonymous core
  by which I know myself.

Jarring Concerns

Aspirations, open-lidded,
  thrust into oblique gray.

Ideas, poems, possibilities invited
  briefly flash colors, illuminate patches,
  then fade, unanswered.

Interest unreciprocated.
  My fireflies flown.

No beacons to challenge the fog.
  Isolation returns, gray as nonbeing.

Adrift

Am I monstrous
 to tell rather than weep?

To raft along this opaque stillness,
 glide over without diving in
 without swimming in memories, emotions.

Not knowing how to be
 other than dry,
 but thirsting for tears.

Home Away from Home

Every home I've known drifts away.
 I don't remember where I'm leaving
 by remaining in place, going nowhere.

Dream me into the ether with you.
 Dream me home
 into multiplying rooms in my mind
 no one enters, not even myself.

Doors closed, receding corridors
 of corridors, rooms filled with tears,
 memories I cannot access,
 how your breath felt on my neck,
 how we slept curled together,
 inhaling one another's scent.

All closed now,
 behind doors in corridors,
 none in any home
 I can know as home.

Next Unknown

I am now in a place of which I know nothing.
 A perfect stranger to myself, my surroundings.

I steer clear of hugs, cringe at touch
 even from those I hold affection for.
 My mind screams silent alarms.

Rarely do I glance at myself in mirrors.
 I have no five-year plan.
 Neither reflection nor projection
 attach to anything
 on either side of my skin.

I write ambiguous words,
 create abstract art,
 perhaps to speak of feelings
 I imagine without feeling,
 hiding from myself inside my intellectual self.

I reside within aftermath,
 a desert with no torrents of tears,
 no wailing grief.

I want to cry.
I cannot.
Evaporated memories scream incoherently at night.

Mostly, I am calm, breathing.
This moment, no before, no beyond.

I breathe because nerves demand it.
Drifting half-asleep, trailing yesterday,
I stare into tomorrow's mirror,
looking for signs of rain,
perhaps a storm
moving, unpredictable,
winds whirling.

Do poems count as tears?
Is one permitted to write of mourning
in lieu of mourning
to imagine feelings
instead of feeling them
for those already buried?

How many volumes of poetry
equal the time better spent weeping?

Mercurial memories transport sorrow with happiness,
inseparable missives bound tight,
opened together, bittersweet.

A taste I recall: sour yet happy,
I have you in my life still,

But differently, your stillness
 a presence from within,
  no longer your arms around me.

Now heat radiates from longing
 which embraces forever present,
  forever absent.

Feeling always of forever.
 But not.

In stillness, I gently smile,
 begin to weep.

Appendix

The Thursday Before That Last Friday

I called Liz, Stephen's mom, on the day that his oncologist advised me to let his family know that they should spend the holiday season with him this year, that there likely wouldn't be another. I asked Liz if she and her tribe would like to come in a week and stay for Thanksgiving, and for as much longer as they wished. I should have known the response would be, "Oh, hell no!" They loaded their vehicles, borrowed money for gas, and hit the road immediately, within hours, caravanning from Minneapolis to Chicago to convene en masse in our living room the evening of Thursday, November 14th, which was Stephen's and my fifteenth-year anniversary. They planned to stay through Monday, November 18th, his fiftieth birthday. He was six years younger than I.

That evening saw the house filled with family, strong family. I'd already seen Liz lose one son, over a decade earlier while she was visiting us for a Labor Day weekend. We'd received a phone call; his youngest brother, Eric, troubled Eric, had been gunned down, was now in the Advocate Christ ER at 95th and Cicero, where all the South Side Chicago gunshot wounds went.

The cab driver said prayers as he drove us from the far north to the far south side of Chicago. Just as we entered the family room, the ER physician emerged to announce that Eric had passed. Liz fell to the floor, wailing. Once you've heard a mother wail at the loss of her child, you've heard grief not to be forgotten.

In our home on this evening, all of his remaining siblings, his sister and three brothers, were present with their spouses, along with nieces and nephews, aunts and uncles, and cousins, cousin being the term used to denote anyone who attends the same family reunion as you but it's too complicated to explain why. Two of his cousins, sister and brother, were themselves taking chemo, fighting for life. Stanley, on leave from his good railroad job, had lung cancer. And Carol, who'd risen to become an upper-level financial officer for a well-known bank, was fighting a recent recurrence of breast cancer.

Separately, discretely, I thanked Stanley and Carol for coming that evening, noting that Stephen's cancer was not their cancer, and that his outcome need not be their outcome. "Thank you for that," said Carol. Both survived for several more years.

Stanley's wife, Sylvia, who over the past months had been schooling me with tips for how to help counteract the ravages of chemotherapy, took a great liking to one of my pastel figure drawings hanging in our front room. The model had been a large, strongly built woman, and I'd drawn two strong, black lines against a chocolate brown background to capture her contour.

"What do you call this one?", asked Sylvia.

"Its formal name," I said, "is 'Tina'", then whispered, "which informally, is an acronym for 'Tits and Ass'". Sylvia burst out laughing, then aligned herself in profile so as to fit the lines of Tina's contour.

"That's me," she declared, "I call her 'Sylvia'". "Sylvia", of course, went home with them that evening to hang proudly on one of the walls in their home.

Throughout the evening, people had been casually stepping into the bedroom to visit with Stephen, who was lying in bed. At one point, however, Stephen surprised us all and came walking out to sit on the sofa in the front room. He wanted to make plans for us all to go to one of his favorite restaurants on Monday to celebrate his birthday. His level of strength and enthusiasm made it seem that might almost be feasible. In any case, we said we would.

Twenty-four hours later, at precisely 7 pm on Friday evening, November 15th, he breathed his last breath. I was holding him as the visiting hospice nurse declared him dead, then left me to spend time alone as she gave his family the news, gathering them into the dining room.

Years later, when I could, I would joke that he'd always been determined to stay forever young, having spent a fortune on lotions and potions to do so, so having already seen his family one last time, he'd decided to skip town prior to his fiftieth birthday.

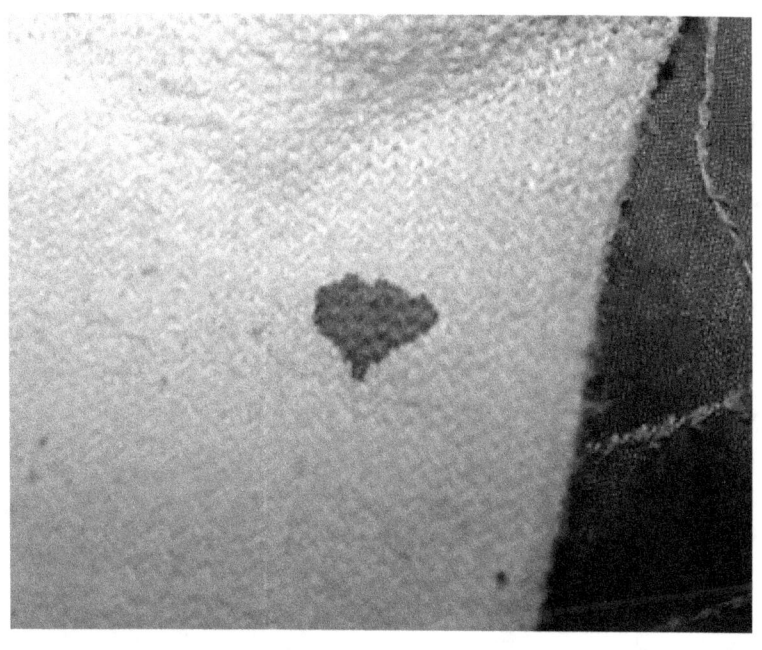

A Perfectly Lovely Mystery

After I returned from the cemetery, I was quickly putting things away to get dressed and ready myself for the work of the day, thankful I don't punch in on a time clock. In the kitchen, I picked up a stack of dingy washrags I'd laundered to re-use as scrub rags. In that pile was a white ankle sock I hadn't intended to use as a rag. I don't know how it got there, but I suspect I might have mistakenly placed it there while folding and sorting my wild, Saturday-night-on-the-town doing laundry this past weekend.

In any event, when I picked it up I noticed a dark red stain and wondered what I could have stepped on to leave that color. Looking more closely, I realized the stain was in the shape of a heart. Closer still, I saw that the "heart" actually had four, rather than two, "shoulders" at the top. Being a bit slow to jump to metaphorical conclusions, I was still puzzling over how such a defined shape could result from stepping on something and what that something might have been as I walked from the kitchen to the bedroom to put the sock away in its drawer.

Here's where the mystery deepens: walking into the bedroom, my eyes focused on the wall where I'd hung memorial photos of the four men with whom, at different times in my life, I'd made plans to share our lives. For all four, those plans were cut short by their untimely deaths. All four are memorialized on our headstone: Stephen on the front, and Jeff, Dennis, and Ben on a plaque mounted on the back. As I made the connection between the four shoulders on the stain of a heart on a sock I was carrying and the four men whose photos hang on my wall, I could swear that I saw the faces in those photos bread into huge smiles. But perhaps that was simply the effect of the tears of joy and sorrow welling up in my eyes.

Rather than "supernatural," I prefer the word *unexplained.* I can't explain how it happened that just after I returned from finalizing the memorial headstone display for the four men I've loved, I would randomly pick up a sock from a pile of rags I'd laundered and find a sharply defined image of a four-shouldered heart in a deep burgundy red, the source of which I cannot identify. I've had all day to think about it, and I still can't explain it. But I can love it, and I don't care whether it ever has an explanation or not.

For me, it is simply a perfectly lovely mystery and a perfectly lovely memory.

If anyone reading this can explain it to me, please don't.

Olive Park Walks (a mantra)

(composed in the spring of 2014 during noontime walks, following Stephen's death on 11/15/2013)

No questions,
 No answers.

No problems,
 No solutions.

No future,
 No past.

No purpose
 but peacefulness.

No time
 but now.

Relax,
 and release.

All is now

 is always
 and never,

is both,
 and neither

is now.
 Step into your own,

and be,
 simply be,

your own, among,
 with.

(if repeating: begin again— "no questions...")

Love the Pain Forward

Not what happened to you
 leave that, leave them,
 where they are, in the past.

But love the pain forward:
 your messenger, your guardian,
 who tells you where the blow landed,
 what got broken, what is different now.

It tells you that you're alive, survived,
 that you have it in you to survive
 even that, even them, their loss.

It tells you that what's broken
 may always be broken,

may always hurt when touched,
that you may always need
to give it extra attention.

But it also tells you
that you have it in you
to survive, to thrive,
to love your life forward.

My Gratitudes

Once there was, and I loved each one.
Now I am, and I remember each one.
I love each one still,
and I am grateful that I can.

So, my life proceeds.

hope and memory
combine in equal measure
life's daily tincture

In the night, dancing
with ghosts, pain signifies touch:
beloved touch, walls.

II. <u>Via</u>

<u>Obliquities</u>

A Philosophical Coming of Age Memoir

Chapters

Chapter 1 — *Isolation*

Chance Encounters

Writing into the intimate, very darkness we attempt to imagine form onto those features our groping fingers find by chance encounter bodies in perpetual motion confuse sweat, exchange odor, maintain rhythm. We ask about integrity: if truth, like light, forever changes appearances, are we better to love in the dark, groping?

Hostile Child

The child is absurdly arrogant and self-righteous, and knowing that, I know he will save me. He believes, has willed himself chosen of God, so I chose him to protect my darker mysteries: my sex and my art. He is not a bad child, and mine was not a bad choice, but time has circumvented the necessity of our arrangements. I've grown, and he's grown restless. I've sensed recently that his anger is beginning to turn against me, and I want to find him before he stops holding his breath out of pride and begins to do so with a more malicious intent. I expect I'd like him, if I could remember more about him.

On the Edge

Or, if we do speak of these things, we use the silences to convey our more precise understandings, would you not agree? On the edge, where we are now thinking, rules do not hold so tightly, and logic crumbles like simple math applied to the physics of infinity. One plus one is an open question, as it turns out.

Why, then, do you ask me the attributes of God? I'd rather we talk about us, and how we'll get along. God is dead; life must go on, and so we do what needs be done. Oh, you would not wonder about God if you were hungry. You'd look for food. Does this answer your question?

Well, then God is everything, that's what. And nothing. Light and dark and all the shades between are God, and everything that happens. Beautiful and ugly are the same is God, no? Yes, this is so, we know, you and I. We think and are conscious and intelligent, but God isn't like that, so we're done with God and can think about other things now.

Sex

Watch we slower our eyes tenderly: contacts like this are not unfamiliar to those of us accustomed to unflinching at the if moment of another male's touch. Up, thrust, collision, action; for every intercourse an equal and similar thrust reaction; into together we each slam our male-mated egos splitting, splitting, anonymous, asunder. Hard cock, your hot cum fuck in me, man; oh man, fuck me down, fuck me netherly down;

down, down, down. In the still, gently afterward lying softly, coming together, scattered issues of everyday life repose.

Honesty

I am not honest, which saddens me, but honesty is no simple matter. I do, however, have an ear for truth and an appreciation of its many shades.

Desert

Enter, enter; here, open lies all this land is sameness, all is plain, open, lying brown in the sun. The dust tells us secrets about this place: like loneliness itself, this place is devious; it crawls with schemes and whispers and desiccates any spirit foreign to its clime.

Spring Song

Wheezing, screaking, dissonant:
 amoral blackbird chorale
 performed from leafless perches,
 plundering the silence, oracle
 of an oaken spring sanctum.

Second Nature

Events resist summation. We speak of particular, peculiar, short-lived lives I've led; hence my body to ashes, my files to psychology.

I've just learned that acid inherent in the materials will disintegrate my art, that the abstract expression of my mind resists endurance. Well, to decline is the second nature of things, I guess, and my guess is no better than yours. You've a knack, it seems, for integrating desire with doing, though I've seen you pause over a question or two of mine, at times.

Fossil Words

I'm imagining myself past the ripple, into the shadow state where I hope soon to meet up with you. We've been apart far too long already; I feel I was born lonely. Did you – question, question, I attempt to regain you by engaging your intellect, imagining your response to my inquiry. Pretend yourself the subject and my purpose for doing this, surmise significance in these worm-trail fossil words. We go crazy in our dreams, but I don't remember mine.

Torsion

Echoes are what they have now: memory's torsion, conning, the subornation of history. What writer does not suborn words, what eye does not suborn the light entering it?

Depths

Most life is lived in shallows by creatures accustomed to light – flashy, sun-accustomed creatures of a social, carnivorous nature, whereas in depths are solitary, here-and-there loners eating plankton. Having been there, I can report there is distance, not mystery, in the depths, except what mystery shallow-dwellers imagine, expecting things not seen to be invisible rather than merely dull.

Rough Lines

Then is one always so fragile in the face of time and circumstance? Heat blurs the air, and a shadow only approximates the object of my desire. What, then, can we assume, or must we assume it all? Is there no balm in Gilead? Oh, we are a strong people, to be sure; we must bleed – Others.

Round and round and round and round our home object turns corners as we scribe our details on its surface, ever fearful, heedless that our little lines will scratch too deeply and the whole inside pour out. Then where would we be? If these lines don't say much to you, well, feel them, they're rough, and I am a little touched. Boo!

Office Job

What constitutes a thought, do you know? Well, one needn't bother with every little distraction, or one would never begin, would one? Blood — no, the word attracts the wrong crowd; we must be more circumspect. Can one have done something, committed an act, say, without having thought about it, even at the time? Oh, everyone has a story or more to tell, as if the telling somehow validates the things done. Minds and deeds are murky; one must recall.

Tension wires the stories. She noticed a piece of lint on his jacket as her friend was showing them the new office space and casually picked it off. Her friend observed the entirety of this action then almost immediately dismissed it as if it were perfectly innocuous, but did so a bit too intently — and that is why I, observing them, suspect she and he are romantically involved. This was in a story I once read, but I tell you I saw it happen. I could give you their names.

Why are you reading this? Do you enjoy watching a worm exposed to the sun? How, then, can one distinguish between imagination and reality? Here, a scene from music camp flashes past: the smell of the cabins with clean, young bodies and musical instruments, and there were bunk beds. But nothing happened on the porch of the big dormitory on the hill overlooking the lake. Nothing happened in that room, which I vaguely remember passing through, which still fascinates me with its wood-burning stove and a musty smell that even now I can distinctly recall.

Mary's arm lingered in the pool. Her half-distracted, half-hearted "thank you" trailed a baited question mark, inviting the ennui-inclined sucker to test her lines; skin is such fun, you know? I like to touch inside skin, the underpart of things.

Then the nervous rattle of keys and coins in his pocket as they say goodbye at least ten times — his employment taking him to another town; she has a call on hold. Will they remain friends? Do you ever wonder what's happening now, or are you the next to nothing to go a sanguineous good-bye?

So? Why this fascination? Did it happen, or was it a picture I made? I'm writing this at my desk as I thought that would be better for appearances' sake. You understand, don't you?

Dream #3

I am digging the black jelly rot out from inside knotholes and under the bark of a young tree, using a silver soup spoon, unsure whether the tree will survive.

Logic

I wish to tell you of my personal experience, the falling apart of logic, all cause belied by being, every word foolish on my tongue, every memory an acidic gurgle. Always there is a dishonesty present in what is the case; even now I have lied. I don't stop lying when I admit the truth, this stultifying fear of getting at the untruth I fear I am.

Chapter 2 — *Despair*

Childhood Dream

I do not awaken with any recollection of having had
nightmares. I remember many of my dreams when I was a
young child were of escaping down earthen tunnels to another
world, remote and completely different, filled with marvelous
machinery; or of sneaking into a cemetery and burying the
body of someone I'd killed (who? accidentally?) inside a vault,
atop the body of an old woman I didn't know, who had
recently been buried there, then waking terrified that those
who had buried her would return, discover the vault had been
disturbed, and that my crime would be discovered.

Cat Dream

Cut open the living cat and eat its candy bones – this the
message from the dream: no pain, all is pleasant, but the cat
dies.

Leaving a Mess

I feel so tired, incapable of sustained intellectual activity. I'm
trying to think through questions of what I want to

accomplish with my art. This morning I sat on the floor by the refrigerator and beat my head with my fists until I saw stars. I'd just come in from trying to figure out how to change the windshield wiper blades, which had frustrated me. I think the only way I'd ever actually kill myself would be if I could do so on impulse, but I want to arrange things, tie up loose ends, plan the event so as to allow people to consider it an accident. I wonder: do real artists really have, pursue lofty ideas, or is it all just coping with stress? I shouldn't be writing this, for fear someone might find it and read it after. I don't want to leave a mess behind.

Non-presence

The only solution seems to be to sit very quietly, to allow no thought, no idea or memory to intrude, to be very, very still so that nothing happens to cause me to think. This is how most people know me: on autopilot, withdrawn, a benign non-presence onto which they can project their own imaginings of me. My secret is that I don't exist; I am a product of every imagination but my own.

Part Apart

Time between, apart,
isolated.
Future motion in the presence of the past,
in the company of, but
unconnected.

An organism evolved beyond its environment,
with vision that encompasses
but voice that lacks hearing
so it observes, continually,
in solitude,
bemused as it watches itself function
in a world of which it cannot be a part
from which it cannot be apart.

Contradictory Demands

Some lies hurt more than others; I, for instance, frequently cripple but rarely kill outright. What we must realize as we become older is how the thing-in-itself of our strong words like honor, truth, or murder is mere description and embarrassing to those of us who might have attributed to them more profound, metaphysical meanings. Therefore, it follows that civilization is a membrane frequently punctured, rarely torn. In my neighborhood is an old derelict whom I have befriended and whom I intend to kill.

He desires this, though he hasn't said so in as many words, and I envisage his going off to his final sleep as I cradle his head in my lap, gently nudging away his resistance to the release. I will report the crime and stay with the body until the police arrive to take us into their care. I do not wish death for myself at this time; rather, I intend to resolve through his release the contradictory demands placed upon me by my love and my art as manifested in my too little life for both.

Freedom, prison, deprivation – I am an artist; I draw pain. Of all other responsibilities I must relieve himself.

What concerns us here is the mood of fragmentation in modern society, or if it is even possible to exist at the level of words anymore. Our thoughts at this juncture are like the passing in opposite directions of two yellow automobiles, one an old Checker cab still in commerce and the other, somewhat more pale in hue, a private pleasure vehicle.

Virus

In my bloodstream my last journal is completed, locked, without key; the question pertains to the date on the last entry, and why it should matter. My mistake was to project the significance of my existence into the future, to pursue possibilities sprung from my imagined life and overlook my more real potential to be someone you might know now.

Ultimate Answer

No, I don't believe that my life is necessary. What I believe is that my life happened, is happening. That I know. There is no why, no ultimate answer. All there is is this life, these circumstances. If I attempt to invest my life with meaning I fail because there is no meaning, just a record, more or less accurate. The chapters cannot be unwritten; what I've allowed in the name of a higher cause has neither justification nor remedy, but undeniable repercussions.

Shards

We are now so many pieces. How many times did the hammer
fall, reverberate with each blow? Each time you blink, I recall
the pain, and if you turn your head, and if I speak of
bloodletting, is there no higher purpose than memory? What
do you want of me, my friend? Can you make sense of it all?
I'd like to hear what you've to say for yourself, and I'll watch
your face, carefully. We are not necessary, but an option. Each
spring one must wonder at it all, and if it's our last flowering.
Are we always to see only the water's surface, stirred by things
beneath, reflecting things above — good God, we are beasts of
desire, what more do we want? Hit the damn mirror, then,
and feel it splash.

Abyss

We are all walking along the abyss; some slip, we pull them
out, then throw them back over.

At a Loss

Time without word coming, I'm waiting through a few more
moments of void; dropping into the ashtray are stories
aborted, willed distractions. This kind of pain must negate
language, or we'd have common words for it by now, like
anxiety, only more specific.

Where the spine joins the head: tightness, throbbing tension,
unrelieved, caged, caged, implosive words unsaid. We are

losing the sense of it; we are losing – alone, finding myself alone, I, finding myself alone, I sat for a chat? No, I, bereaved expatriate talk is of how we were; people define our definitions, take us away. Finding myself alone, I observe: an inability to concentrate, effect, dispose, communicate, connect with particles of ideas. Nothingness makes sense. I can tell you about this pain he feels, and I cannot touch it, this throbbing tightness where the spine joins the head, these too many thoughts filling the brain, seeping out, spoiling, poisoning down the neck, turning muscle into a meaningless, ineffectual nothingness. I fear I am speaking now to those who wondered what I meant by my not saying. Newly conversant with death and loss, I discover a whole new litany of unresolved rage. Amen.

Dirt

We are never far from dirt creeps up on us from under our fingernails we scrub back the dirt, but it wins.

Ants

Recall defects; in memory, lies. Or perhaps thought happens like that damp, warm spot one must see to understand is one's own blood. Here's a rule of husbandry: beware lest you think the words too deeply. Or he was my best first love. Still, in the sense that one's endeavors are poetry and nothing more, a fiction like all art, I wonder: do the peonies with the ants still bloom?

Memory

In my memory, vague and whispery, are all the plans, the many storylines I am, the tomorrow's task I am trying to recall.

Chapter 3 --
Ambivalence

Icarus

Slower move the eyes, blink
 my mind into a deeper unknowing.

Up against this loss we rage
 creative against nature's viral
 decimation thrust human endeavor,
 or what of all our futures' history?

Nor was he afraid of fire.
 Then are we now burning
 our brains with why?

If we do nothing there is no why,
 only loss and loss.

But at the speed of light, effect is cause;
 what comes of this death is why

another candle and another and another
 flames must flame.

If to the moon, why not another sunrise?

Collective

For whom does one speak
  when speaking of our kind?

We who weave of ourselves an identity,
  an entity collective, planting the mustard seed
  that moves mountains, leaving a whole
  where our name was.

Everything has its cost.

Purpose

But it has, nonetheless,
  served some purpose.

I am not altogether lost.
  Would you care to chat,
  go for a walk, perhaps?

Why are these silences
  so deeply still? Has it been so long?

I am not familiar with this feeling
  something coming together,
  emerging from the frantic whirl of pieces.
  There is a thing taking shape at the center,
  growing a purpose?

All right, all right,
  my part is to listen.

Emergence

Pulling together,
 the initiative from within,
 definition emerges.

I must speak my peace of mind;
 it will not be told to me.

Isolation

Do you know how lonely I am,
 or why?

Yes, I am quiet,
 and I am lonely inside my silence.

If one is an artist, if one creates,
 one must have friends.

The isolation creativity creates
 requires connection to relieve the pain.

Statement

My art is the spontaneous, emotive expression
of the concerns in my life.

Its validity is contingent upon the scope, depth,
and integrity of my response to life.

I hope people respond to my work intuitively,
and in so doing recognize something
of themselves in it.

Once Upon an Angst

"Once upon an angst, there was this little child
lost in a big woods. He'd wandered there
well, actually he'd run, in order to escape
his parents, which is a pretty normal thing
for children of his age to do, and a good thing, too..."

Someday I may want to recall these moments.
Perhaps then I will better understand them,
or at least look back at what might have been.
At present, I record. If by recording I create,
well, then we shall see.

"...So here he was in the middle of a big woods,
shadows everywhere and a little bit of everything
he'd ever wondered about. At his parents' house
(which he refused to call home anymore, though

it took vigilant effort not to slip) he used to climb
trees in the yard to see further, beyond the place
where his parents lived. Here in the forest
there were many, many trees.

His question was: which one to climb first,
if any at all? The decision had taken
considerable pausing over, and he'd made
a brave start or two, but hadn't really
gotten very far. The tops didn't look
so inviting once he'd begun..."

At some point, it behooves us to note
that we are becoming, are something.

Our preoccupation with "what shall I be?"
loses urgency.

We realize our complexity and being something
no longer provides the easy answer to life's mystery,
no longer promises unmitigated belonging,
worthiness, or the necessity of participation
because something larger than ourselves has decreed it.

At those times we can risk understanding ourselves.
Or we can opt out, enjoining suicide, insanity,
mediocrity, or aggression to dissipate our momentum.

"...In his wanderings, he came to a meadow
where all the growing things were new and familiar.
The trees from which he'd emerged were no longer
so tall, nor the brush so hostile.

It was his meadow, he knew,
 and he set out to explore it
 and create for himself a home."

It does not seem so strange anymore,
 not to have answers, nor so incumbent
 upon us to ask other people's questions.

Ah, but we are still curious
 and curiosity is a wonderful thing,
 and comfortable, too.

Compromise

No longer pushing out against circumferences,
 our now-minimal, mid-life selves are redrawn.

In this line of thought we are contained,
 more aware of our frame of reference.

We are a dialectic of aspiration and reflection,
 urge and knowledge, comprehension
 of outer limitations and recognition
 of depths within ordinary spaces.

Ordinary spaces, whose boundaries
 we once thought to break,
 but are content now merely to have found.

Perhaps what we have here
 is that which we were once young enough
 to disdain as compromise.

Integration

How does one describe the process
 by which we come to terms with life,
 by which we integrate ourselves with the whole,
 by which we come to accept the complexity,
 the vast and varied stuff of living,
 the process by which we begin to learn
 from those who disagree fundamentally
 with our being?

Of course we give up dreams
 to grasp hold of reality,
 yet we retain our dreams too.

It's a curiosity how those dreams
 become more possible
 when we leave them alone.

Do I make sense to you?
 Have we been here before,
 gone through this together?

I love him.
 And he knows that.

Chapter 4: *Settling into Myself*

Dear Millie and Dick,

Yes, of course, I have always known and valued the special place you've made in your hearts for me. How could I forget always wanting to stay with you when my sisters went to Edith and Lloyd's, or playing with Thumper, watching you wax Karen's Homecoming roses, the birds you always fed (in spite of the squirrels), the time I wet my bed at your place and felt so bad, but especially just taking in the warmth and love you shared with me, and the joy you both have always taken in life and found in each other.

I still keep the little stuffed black dog you gave me when I was in the hospital with pneumonia way back in the first grade, and Dick's woodcarving greets me every morning with fond recollections. You two and your family have been more of a role model for me than you might ever have imagined.

I especially value the support and joy you've given my parents over the years. On one of the most difficult days of my life, on the day after I'd told my parents of my being gay and of my break with their spiritual beliefs, I'd come to the house to get my belongings in order to move to Cloquet for the summer. I'd left my mother extremely distraught and in tears, and on my way to the freeway I passed you going rapidly and grim-faced in the opposite direction. I've always hoped that my mother had called you, and that you were on your way to give her support and comfort.

I do very much appreciate and take seriously your concern for my physical and spiritual well-being. I am enclosing copies of letters I have sent to my brothers with the hope that they will help you put to rest the burden you feel for me. You cannot imagine how deeply I feel for those gay people who see their sexuality as an impediment to their spirituality, who try to soothe the estrangement they feel from God and family with obsessive sex, drugs, alcohol, overextended credit, whatever. All gay life is not like that, and no gay life should need to be like that.

I am glad for the author of the article you sent that he was able to come to an understanding and forgiving spiritual peace before he died, and I hope you will understand that I have also come to an equally profound, if somewhat different, spiritual peace in my life.

With best wishes for a joyous holiday season, and love and respect for you always,

Philip

Dear Joel,

I hope you won't mind that I am enclosing with this letter a letter I've written to Basil. He had written to me with many of the same concerns you've expressed, and I wrote my response with both of you in mind. At the end of the letter to Basil, I'll add a few sentences in response to specific concerns you expressed in your letter.

First, however, I must give you some "big brotherly" words of encouragement. At the end of your letter you say that you have never been a strong speaker, and that it is difficult for you to put emotions into words. I found your letter to be evidence quite to the contrary. Your writing is eloquent, forcible, forthright, thoughtful, and logically structured far in advance of what I would expect from someone your age. You have a gift for communication, at least in the written word (speaking spontaneously is difficult for me too), and I must encourage you to develop that talent. It may be that I might oppose the use to which you put that talent, but I am completely in favor of and will always respect your putting it to use.

Well, read my letter to Basil, and then we'll see if perhaps we can at least come to a respectful understanding of each other.

Dear Basil,

At long last I am responding to your letter of last February 15th. I had written you a letter dated 2/24, but then decided not to send it until you'd had the "Philosophy of God" course you'd mentioned. Then I got involved in my painting class, etc., etc., and just haven't taken the time to update that letter and get it sent. Today a cold is forcing me to take a break from my painting, so I'm finally getting my letter writing done.

I guess I've put off finishing my response to your letter because I've already settled those issues of spirituality and sexuality, and they've become an integral part of what I am. I tend to want to get on with life, to do and celebrate my relationship with God rather than to pick apart and analyze what that relationship is. My art is so important to me because it's an expression of my spirituality; it's the putting into action of my beliefs, a part of my prayer and meditation time, if you will.

I want you to understand that I do not reject your spirituality, and I do not want to argue you away from your beliefs in favor of my own. You are your own person with your own circumstances and needs that your spirituality must address. Rather, I hope that by understanding my beliefs, you will be able to make room for me in your belief system as I've made room for you in mine, and that you will feel as deeply at peace in your beliefs as I feel in mine.

Like you, I began to have serious spiritual doubts in my teens. Mostly, I couldn't bring myself to believe that we as born-again Christians were the only ones going to heaven, and that the rest of the people throughout the world, throughout history, would go to hell. That began a whole series of questions and self-discoveries, including the reconciliation of my sexuality with my spirituality, which brought me around to where I am now—not rejecting God or Christianity, but taking issue with Christianity's exclusive claim on God.

Fundamentally, I believe we are all part of God happening, and that we're each responsible for how our own little bit of

God happens, and for how it connects with the rest of God happening. Philosophically, I think of God as a verb rather than a noun. God is what the universe, known and unknown, does (matter is energy is motion; instead of an unmoved mover, the mover and moved are one). I think the religious impulse is an instinctive call to participate in creation, a survival instinct for ourselves and our species. Words like *good* and *perfect* describe the human desire to exist and perpetuate ourselves; they are the tools with which we order our existence. Good and evil exist only from a human perspective. Were we to annihilate ourselves, God/the universe would continue to be. It is left to our own free will as a species to choose to continue to be a part of the great mystery of God unfolding.

People have responded to the spiritual impulse to exist in many different ways. Out of the richness of history, different religions have emerged, each with many variations and all possessing strengths and weaknesses relative to each other. Religious practice and theology need to accommodate individual and cultural psychologies. The Hebrew tradition reflects the needs of a small tribe invading a fertile land, and the Hindu tradition reflects the needs of ordering a huge population in a barren land.

Virtually all religions throughout history have bestowed on God some sort of human face whether that face be benevolent, terrible, wise, vengeful, whatever, and many have given God many faces. In order to feel a personal relationship with God, many people find it effective to imagine God with human attributes and values (kindness, justice, etc.). I don't think that is necessarily wrong, so long as it is acknowledged that the various stories are means of getting a grasp on truth and not the ultimate truth in themselves.

Through their sacred stories, various religions teach us different methods of connecting ourselves with the rest of God happening. Which, if any, of these methods are appropriate for our lives is something we can only choose for ourselves. There are always those people who work out their spirituality apart from any organized religion or set of beliefs.

Personally, I've felt most at home spiritually, most closely connected with God in the Unitarian-Universalist denomination because it makes room for the great diversity of religious expression. And, as I said, I've found that creating artwork is how I am best able to enact God in my own life (though I don't think of making art as any more exalted a calling than, say, fixing cars or programming computers).

I understand and fully respect your choice to connect with God through the born-again Christian tradition. Now, one aspect of that tradition is its tendency to compete with other religions by condemning them, just as fundamentalist factions in most of the world's religions do, and of course I must oppose that belief because it affects me politically and encourages a societal attitude which puts me in physical danger. I would like to think your communion with God through Jesus would be sufficiently rewarding in itself without condemning those outside your tradition to hell both in this life as well as in any afterlife.

Many Christians maintain their deep faith by allowing for variable interpretations of Biblical passages, for instance reconciling their belief in a divinely guided creation per *Genesis* with evidence supporting the evolutionary process. Perhaps you will find that the less narrow and rigid is your interpretation of the Bible, the greater will be your appreciation of its wisdom as it addresses the great universal questions of existence. Personally, I've come to regard the doctrine of hell as a metaphor for the suffering we feel in this life when we are separated from participating to our full potential in the process of God happening, and as a warning for us as a species against the possibility of our annihilating ourselves in a literal lake of nuclear fire.

Well, I'll leave it to you to work out the specifics of your beliefs. My purpose in writing this is not to argue but to show you how we can make room for each other, and to convince you that you need not worry about my spiritual well-being. Or for the quality of my life, for that matter. I am fulfilled in my artistic endeavors, and I have had the very happy fortune to share my life with a wonderful, caring, and thoughtful man for the past six and a half years.

Being the person I am, and especially the gay person I am, I demand of myself and society that I be able to live a moral, decent, and spiritual life. Not necessarily according to any rigid set of rules, but so that my life will improve the quality of life overall. I believe that accepting and celebrating my gayness lends itself to that ethos. Diversity in sexual orientation is a natural part of the richness in the vast scheme of life; the healthy role of a minority population is to enrich and complement the majority population, to play an enlivening counterpoint to the main theme.

I know it might take a stretch for you to accept that, but I hope you are able to do so. Given the reality of the AIDS epidemic, I have had the opportunity to come to a very real recognition of my own mortality. I could die of AIDS, but then, I could be run over by a truck, or I might live to a happy and ripe old age. Whatever my fate, I am content to know what I know about myself.

Best wishes for your endeavors, and I know we'll have the opportunity to talk of our daily doings over the holiday season.

Philip

So, Joel, that pretty well sets out where I am spiritually. I'll just add a bit of personal biography in response to the specific questions you asked.

From as early as I can remember, I felt the way about some of my boyhood friends that most of the boys seemed to feel about special girls, i.e., I got "crushes" on them. I tried not to pay much attention to those feelings, concentrating instead on trying to be a good Christian witness, and throughout high school I was very well respected and had very few friends, because I wasn't much fun to be around. I would allow myself romantic, even sexual fantasies about these boys, but I always imagined them with some anonymous girl, never with myself; nonetheless I'd feel guilty because I thought that thinking about sex was sinful.

My last years in high school and my college years were a time of turbulent rebellion, wanting to break from the religious tradition I'd grown up in but not knowing what to replace it with. In college I studied theater, the classics, philosophy, and was exposed to many different outlooks on life. A couple of plays, *The Children's Hour* by Lillian Hellman and *Boys in the Band* by Mart Crowley raised the concept of homosexuality, though not in that pretty a light; nonetheless, something inside me clicked. I'd had sexual experiences with women, and while I'd enjoyed them, there was still a sexual yearning within me which I couldn't describe but which I knew hadn't been satisfied.

During this time, my spiritual questions brought me to the beginnings of the understanding of religion and spirituality that I described in my letter to Basil. Actually, it was at home during the Christmas break of my junior year, as I was taking a moonlit walk down the road in front of our house, that I had an epiphany of sorts: everything just clicked and made sense to me, and I went back to the house and wrote page after page of notes outlining my newly formulated beliefs.

About a month previous to that, I'd had my first homosexual experience, and it had seemed just so incredibly right and peaceful for me that I knew I'd found a part of my life I hadn't recognized before. Once I'd begun to make sense of my spirituality, I felt secure enough to explore my sexuality. Of course, I still had a lot of maturing and coming to terms with life left to do, but at least I'd found my starting point.

I know that my rebellious period caused a good deal of grief and worry for our parents, and that it's been difficult for all of you as my siblings to understand how I could grow into an outlook on life so different from your own. I've written a number of letters such as these that I'm writing to you and Basil, attempting to set a basis for some understanding. My position is that you need not worry about my spiritual well-being. If you do so, that is your choice, and while I might regret your worry, as well as the familial estrangement it entails, I cannot feel responsible for it.

I don't think it necessary for you to be ashamed to speak of me or of what I am. I'm not. I do wish circumstances could have been different and we could have gotten to know each other better while you were growing up, but life isn't always how we wish it could be. And of course, there's still time. I know that some in the family continue to hurt and worry over me, but I continue to hope that time will allay their fears. I've sensed that with each visit home they are more comfortable around me.

Others in the family have been able to make room for me in their personal belief systems, for which I am grateful, but I do not value my relationship with them any more than I do with those who haven't. You are all my family, and I love and care for each of you in a way unique to who you are.

Take care of yourself, develop your talent for the written word (your voice and stature have great resonance too, should you decide to go into audio or visual broadcasting), and I'm sure we'll be able to talk more of the day-to-day events of our lives during the holiday season.

Sincerely,
Philip

Letter #1 to Pastor Al

Dear Pastor Al,

Enclosed are two poems I've written in response to your messages from the past couple of Sundays. The second, in particular, is a response to your account of your gay brother and your ministry to transvestite prostitutes this past Sunday.

I don't know whether or not you'll agree with the beliefs I express in these poems, but I hope you're comfortable having people who hold these beliefs attend your services. My partner and I have appreciated hearing your message about the all-encompassing nature of God's love, as well as seeing the diversity of your congregation.

The Word

God speaks to us
 with but one word,
 written and spoken as many,
 in many languages,
 using many voices,
 each one imperfect,

human like our own,
so as to engage
our hearts and minds
in listening
ever more closely
for that one pure word,
for the perfect enunciation
of love,
which we sometimes hear
as the whispered echo
of all our talk
about our beliefs.

Lament for Paul

In the Bible,
  the man who wrote
  that homosexuals
  would never inherit
  the kingdom of God
  also wrote
  that woman was created
  for the sake of man,
  that women are forbidden
  from teaching men,
  and from braiding their hair
  or wearing gold and pearls
  or costly garments.

That same man
  wrote that long hair
  is the glory of a woman
  but the shame of a man
  as if God,
  who loves us
  down to the very number
  of hairs on our head,
  will judge us
  based on the length
  we choose to wear them.

That man, I believe,
  had a problem:
  understanding that masculinity
  does not require
  the subjugation of women.

Despite Paul's declaration
  that love for one's neighbor,
  of itself,
  fulfills God's law,

despite his advice
  that nothing in itself
  is unclean, but only
  if it prevents us
  from loving our neighbor,

despite his admonition
  that we neither judge others

nor allow what is good for us
to be spoken of as evil,

still Paul clung
to many of the old rules,
rules that for so long
have separated people
from God's love
so that to this day,
gay people, sadly,
are often better off
saved from a church
instead of in one.

References: Romans 13:8–10; Romans 14:10–18; 1 Corinthians 6:9–10; 1 Corinthians 11:2–15; 1 Timothy 2:9–15.

Letter #2 to Pastor Al

Dear Pastor Al,

Almost you persuaded me to join the men at the altar today for the closing prayer, but a quiet voice inside me told me to hold back. As I sat in the pew, with the women standing around me, I began softly to chide myself for not being able to let go of my deeply ingrained practice of inward, contemplative spirituality and embrace the communal exuberance of the Spirit in your church.

Then, in the midst of the prayer, you spoke words that greatly troubled me, and I realized why I had been guided not to be at the altar. You petitioned God for strength for the men to take a stand against homosexuality, a prayer endorsed by a number of "amens" from the congregation. At that point, I felt the joy of discovering a loving community of worshippers withdrawn from me. I realized I might never again be able to fully trust the expressions of warmth and welcome I had experienced from your congregation.

I realize my departure from your services would not be a significant loss to your church. Obviously your pews are filled with many people who do fully experience the loving embrace of God there. I do, however, fear for the gay children of the congregation who, like me in my youth, may feel led to rebel against the message of God's love because they are taught that what they know themselves to be is unacceptable to their parents, their church, and the God they are encouraged to worship. They may seek to numb the pain of this loss through obsessions with drugs, alcohol, sex, or other hedonistic pursuits. The anger they will feel at their rejection may lead to bitter, cynical lives and tortured relationships. Sadly, there may be few avenues back to God that will embrace them as legitimately gifted by God to be different from the norm.

One knows a perversion because it does not allow its practitioner to love his or her fellow human with the dignity and respect that the love of God affords to every person. I realize there are many perversions to which alienated gay people fall prey, but I also know from God's work in my own life, and the lives of other gay people I've met, that homosexuality itself does not prevent one from embracing others in consonance with God's divine love.

Because we are all human and fallible, we will probably always disagree on some points about how God's word applies to our lives. But I believe God works through our creative, loving conflict to bring us closer and closer to a more perfect understanding of divine love. As the human family has slowly progressed beyond the universal acceptance of slavery (though the number of humans still in bondage in our present-day world is astonishing), I hope it will likewise eventually progress beyond the rejection of its gay relatives to an acceptance that God has a purpose for creating some of us this way.

Whether or not we ever agree on this issue, and whether or not I ever visit your church again, please know that I respect the integrity and compassion of your vision as a minister. I hope that by sharing my thoughts I might persuade you to at least open the door to considering the possibility of full acceptance should someone close to you, perhaps even one of your own children, come to you and say, *"I'm gay, and God made me that way."*

How I Believe

If I believe,
 I do not assert
 that what I believe
 is true,
 and everything else
 is false.

If I believe,
I try to live in accord
with that which, to me,
seems most accurate
in more ways more often
than not,
though that
can change, in which case
I can change what I believe.

If I believe anything, I believe
that the deeper one thinks
into one's beliefs,
the more questions one will have
about them
and the better one will be able
to appreciate beliefs
that differ from one's own,
along with the people who hold them.

I believe we may become wiser,
more humane, more certain
of ourselves, as we understand
our beliefs are likely not
without some degree of error,
that our mortal brains are not built
to comprehend everything
about anything.

Enduring peace is only possible
when people of differing beliefs

meet on the common ground
of a certain ambivalence.

Peace isn't based so much
on what we have in common
as it is on understanding
what we don't
and seeing our differences
as beneficial.

We are not all the same,
do not all want the same things,
do not think the same things.
Our brains do not even
all use the same mechanisms
to gather and process perceptions,
to cogitate cognitions.

The way I think,
such diversity
of thought,
of ways of thinking thoughts
strengthens life,
enriches and renews our own,
along with that of all the life around us.

We do all live on the same,
despite our disparity of abundance,
planet Earth.

Creative Rage

*"And Sophia, the Spirit of God, Wisdom, raged across the face
of the waters."*

Every act of love
  is an act of creative rage
  against the annihilation
  of our species.

The many and varied ways
  by which we express love
  are all manifestations
  of our survival instinct.

Sometimes we love evil,
  mistaking promises of profit
  or fleeting, addictive pleasures
  for actual benefit.

Our errors of choice
  in the objects of our desires
  do not diminish the power
  of our love, only its worth.

Suffering from wrong choices
  allows us to learn
  how better to love the good,
  that which promotes our existence.

With wisdom comes power
  to rage our protective love

for our communal well-being
against all that diminishes life.

Quantum Theology

God is good
  when we are good,
  and God is evil
  when we are evil,
  but mostly
  God is neither.

Good and evil
  are human values.

God is the action
  of every possibility
  becoming.

Whatever might be
  already exists
  in the infinity
  of God becoming.

By our choices,
  our actions,
  prayers and thoughts,
  we influence
  which one
  of all the possible worlds

we will experience
as our own.

Good is what promotes
our existence.
Evil inhibits us.

If we choose
good enough,
our possible existence
continues to become.

The human endeavor
is to connect
with that part of God
in which we thrive.

God's Ugly Voice

Sometimes God happens
through the murderer
who has molested our children
before killing them.

At these times we cry:
How is this possible?
That this is human?
That this is a part of God
becoming like ourselves?

Sometimes God happens
through earthquakes,

disease, floods, and volcanoes.
Injured, we pull back and ask:
Why does God become like this?

Instead, we might ask:
 How might we have known?
 And what might we have done
 to prevent this part of God
 from happening this way?

Sometimes God approaches us
 through disagreeable people,
 burdening our lives
 with jealousy, envy, and discord.

Then we must ask ourselves:
 How might we best love this God,
 becoming manifest in this person,
 so that each of us might invest
 our better selves into developing God?

God doesn't exist
 in perfection,
 rather as dynamic,
 in perpetual motion,
 as a kinetic process of becoming.

What moves God
 is the desire of all things
 to thrive, to become.

As such, God exists in each of us
and everything around us,
whether beautiful
or ugly.

Our hope as a species
is to improve how God exists
through our efforts
to improve our collective lives,
through our instinctual reach for wisdom.

Theology for Lovers

(for Charles Stephen Hughes)

If we hear God becoming
through the sounds
we hear around us,
then your voice,
resonating in my ears,
is how most often
I hear God speaking.

If we feel God becoming
through the hands of others,
then your arms around me
in the comfort of our bed,
in the sanctity of our home,
or in public testimony
feel to me of God's caresses.

If we live within the time and space
 of God becoming in our lives,
 then the time and space I share
 with you in our world,
 the coordinates of you
 that I keep in my mind,
 place me already in heaven.

If you represent God's love to me,
 then I, too, have the opportunity
 to surround you with my love
 so that you, too, may experience
 God becoming better for us
 whenever you think of me.

Our love becomes our most intimate,
 most important knowledge of love,
 the engine of God becoming, benefitting
 beyond our entire species, our entire world.

I Am I That I Am We

This part I call myself
 covers us like a skin,
 moves in the space where
 memory and expectation
 come near enough to each other
 to feel clear, known, present.

As if in a space that could exist
 unto itself,

as if in a self that could exist
unto itself,
among other selves existing
unto themselves,
forgetting, ignoring
that we all exist together,

That we are all what little is known,
along with all that is unknown;
that the "I" that is known
can only exist in relationship to,
as a part of, the other that is unknown;
that I and my every other, is we.

Which is how we might understand
what some of us might call God,
what all of us know beyond what we know,
but see in our each and every other,
connected in ways known and unknown,
the interconnected we which encompasses us all.

Self-Preservation

Self is the skin of our being,
that part we present to one another
to distinguish our particular function,
informing how we might best fit
to function together as one.

Beneath the self runs connective tissue,
pulling together myriad threads

ancestral genetics going back
to life's first imprint, going forward
to the merging of our parents' DNA.

Current and residual ways of perception,
embedded in words, syntax, grammar,
signs and gestures communicating
with one another throughout our world
all one, all made from common elements.

The dust of stars arranged this way and that,
yet all the same dust, the same blips of energy,
constituents of interconnected being,
reliant on the well-being of one another,
signaling from the skins of our particular selves.

Rock, soil, air, water, vegetative, animal
all the in-between categories, cultures,
times, geographies, assumptions
signaling all we hold in common,
all that we must work together to protect.

Walking Along

So many paths, these past few years,
made by walking
in the shoes
(or their semi-functional remains)
of others, also still or recently homeless,

Yet able and generous enough
 to share their stories, to feed my poetry,
 give sustenance, strength
 to my own feet, clad second-hand,
 walking alongside theirs.

So many stories, so many lives,
 paths I could not have imagined
 had I not also happened to stumble
 over my particular stones of grief and despair,
 each of us having our own,

Happened to fall alongside the path,
 as others I had known kept walking,
 while I curled up, kept quiet, rolled
 out of sight.

As they kept walking their paths,
 I found myself walking a path with others,
 unknown, in homeless shelters
 whose missions mostly were to save
 our souls, but along the way
 did provide food, clothing, used soles,
 a place to stop, rest, pause, shower.

Guardedly, we shared our stories,
 recollecting our disparate selves,
 sharing them carefully, haltingly
 with one another, knowing this audience
 to be the few able to comprehend context.

Chapter 5 –
Beginnings & Endings

My mind shatters into fragments,
 each with several cutting edges
 past, present, future, and imagined.

Commotion, the noise of people,
 being around people, often
 I want to scream.
 Instead, I shut down, go vacant.
 Usually.

I still scream in public sometimes,
 but most often at home, by myself.
 Slivers, blips, fragments of memories flash
 feelings of commotion.
 I feel inadequate, overwhelmed,
 ashamed of myself,
 humiliated though by what, I do not know.

I live in a space distanced from myself,
 lose track of pronouns when giving accounts of my life,

use *he*, *you*, *I*, and *they* interchangeably
especially in my thoughts, sometimes in my speech.
Psychologists likely have a term for this,
but I have never done well with therapy.

I've made half a dozen attempts I can recall,
but always "failed to form a therapeutic alliance."
In the original, handwritten draft
I began this very paragraph with:
"He lives in a space distanced from myself..."

Priming the Pump,
Attempting to Remember

I awaken to myself spewing a cacophony
pinched, piercing, nonsensical chatter,
a mishmash of negative vitriol cut and spliced
into so mad an array as to evidence no meaning
beyond that of a feral beast snarling,
wounded and cornered.

This has become a recurring feature of my nights,
the 2:00 a.m. squall of unresolved, traumatic grief.
I inhale deeply, pay attention to my breath,
methodically relax the ligaments in my appendages,
each joint individually: tongue, neck, shoulders,
toes, knuckles, ankles, wrists, elbows, knees, vertebrae.

I sing vibrating monosyllables,
ah, *om* into my agitation.
I start to relax, easing back toward sleep.

But then my mind spins kaleidoscopically again,
churning with images composed
of free-floating anxieties, agitations
detached, abstracted, unsourced.

No longer connected to their roots in the soil of lives
that, in waking hours, I might be remembering,
or imagining, dreaming, amalgamating
from scattered remains decomposed together
over the course of sixty-some years of burial.

I hug myself, arms crisscrossed over my chest,
grasp my shoulders, rock my torso.
I assure the child within my chest
that I will look out for him,
do my best to make sure he is safe.
(He always sees through the impossible,
so I am careful not to overpromise.)

I ask if I can hold his hand, perhaps hug him gently,
tell him I'll listen carefully to whatever
he might want to say, whether now or later.
Otherwise, I will just sit with him quietly,
sharing silent company.

Eventually, after perhaps an hour of alternating outbursts
with soothing breathing, surfing
atop crescendos that might feel beyond endurance,

yet I trust to break again and again
because I have ridden them so often,
I eventually calm, return to sleep.

These episodes – neurological tics,
psychological flashbacks,
 or likely some of each,
 occur throughout my days as well.

Their volume ranges from inaudible mutters
 to piercing, full-throated howls of pain
 expressed in words whose meaning, if they carry any,
 remains oblique, even to me.

Their syntax is peculiar, impossible to capture.
 My mind automatically corrects the errors
 as I recall what I've just said.
 The samples I've managed to provide
 to psychologists over the years are meager.

They ask me when I feel happy.
 I say: *I can feel calm, neutral,
 not joy or fun, but dutiful accomplishment.*
 "Relief that that's over"
 is probably my most positive emotional response.

He feels no happiness,
 recognizes pleasant perceptions
 but has no emotional connection to them.
 They inspire no response.

He always appears remarkably calm.
Little is known about him.
How much of this account is memory
must be questioned. I apologize –
Often I live one or two persons removed
from myself. I, you, he, and we are all me, or it.

Should I edit for consistent pronouns?
It feels more honest to leave them
as they first spill onto the page.

He believes he is mostly what he never imagined,
mostly what others imagine him to be.
As such, his brain reports that we are disparate,
inconsistent, continually morphing images
imagined once upon a time, now
recollected from unstable memories,
scattered in pieces,
a mess like everyone's, perhaps
but all that I own.

Much is gone, placed elsewhere.
I cannot recall where elsewhere is.

Home has moved.
The last time I wrote, there was no response.
It had dispersed; I am dispatched, discarded.

Perhaps, for now, we are encapsulated,
hunkered down in dormancy,
waiting to see, or just waiting.

Earliest Memory

The earliest I can recall:
I awaken sweaty, covered in a hot,
yellowish-green-brown paste
the putrid tang of puerile diarrhea,
sour, piercing, sharp,
with a sickly-sweet undertone.

My older sister (eighteen months my elder)
and I were in the crib in my parents' bedroom.
Our newborn sister (twenty months my junior)
must have been in their bed, swaddled.

By that calculus, I would be two years old, perhaps.
Can one recall an event from the second year of life?

This is my undocumented memory of a memory
first written out twenty-five years ago,
already some thirty-five years after the fact.
I'd occasionally recalled it before,
but finally wrote it down because I'd read
that one's earliest memory
reveals how one views one's life overall.

How telling, then, that my earliest memory
is of being covered in shit.

I've never told this to anyone.
Never been one to shit and tell.

Boiling Potatoes

Parboiling, rather,
 in preparation for freezing,
 to thwart spoilage while out of town
 for my father's funeral.

Dead time this afternoon,
 everything packed, waiting

I run financial reports,
 write the Treasurer's report
 for the OffCenter Community Arts
 monthly board meeting,
 which I will miss.

Boiling potatoes, figuring finances
 to bury grief, or to discharge it?

I reconcile my emotions
 by cutting up onions
 to freeze alongside the potatoes,
 both held for cooking later.

For now,
 tears balance life's books.

The Prodigal Returns

For his Father's Funeral

Alone, stark
  unadorned by memory,
  worn through memories of memories,
  threadbare, unstable,
  nothing fit to wear in public,
  best suited to disintegrate
  on the hanger, unworn.

The storyteller stops telling.
  No one left to listen,
  nothing to be heard, anyway.

Leave yourself alone.
  Leave yourself behind. Go on.

Forget the stories you're telling,
  forget the stories you've been told.
  Forget yourself, you've gone
  too far away to remember anyone.

Keep walking.
  No one remembers
  that you are gone
  beyond memory.

Visit.
  Breathe dust.
  Leave.

No Fairy Tale Funeral

9" x 12" pages, black, acid-free, noncorrosive,
 clear acrylic covers protecting, preserving
 images meant to evoke memories, narratives,
 a web of lives connected to my father.

On his memory table rests the photo album:
 a padded, royal-blue cover,
 four inches thick with genealogy.

Spanning the ninety-two years of his life,
 memorialized, remembered, stories told
 images captured from back before cameras lied
 so subtly, convincingly, routinely as they can now.

Manipulated shades of light, perhaps,
 but rare the claims of proof
 of Loch Nessie or Cottingley fairies.

Organized into sections for the generations:
 beginning in grey monotones,
 his parents, my father, three sisters, two brothers
 from infancy on.

Hard work.
 Occasional smiles.
 Mostly posed, solemn.

Growing up on a hog farm.
 4-H, FFA awards.
 High school activities.

Dating my mother, getting serious, enlisting for Korea,
marrying first.

Upon his return, the next section shifts to color:
I and my siblings – five sisters, three brothers, myself.

Each of them with two pages apiece,
 filled top to bottom with photos:
 academics, sports, music, weddings, grandchildren,
 visits home for holidays, deer hunting seasons.

I turn to my pages.
 See one 3-inch square photo: me in sixth grade,
 my crossing guard flag and vest.

Plus four 1-inch cut-outs:
 elementary school to college.

All fit into the upper-left corner of the first page.
 The other page left completely blank.

Empty. True.

No photos of fairies, it seems,
 were to be countenanced
 in this family registry.

Understanding Onions

Our brains are built to tell us stories,
  to perceive, explain our circumstances,
  to construct a storyline in relationship.

Strict rationalists explain coincidence
  as stories our brains throw together,
  more for comfort than to discern
  cause and effect.

The last time I cut up onions for freezing
  was to prevent spoilage
  while away at my father's funeral.
  I wrote a poem telling the story.

This afternoon, while cutting onions once more
  for freezing, I learned
  that my mother was in urgent care
  signs of liver failure.

How many layers to these onions?

No tumors, nothing to biopsy.
  My mind will have free rein tonight,
  storytelling, awaiting tests tomorrow.

A Few, Final Words

Last Monday my mother, after a surprising uptick
in energy and cognition over the weekend,
was decidedly down.

Hospice suspected she may have had a stroke in the night.
She was having difficulty swallowing food or water.

Each subsequent day she was less able
until Wednesday, when hospice advised us
to anticipate her passing within a week to ten days.

Thursday my suspended antigen injections,
chemical castration, were resumed.
Again I began experiencing "manopausal" hot flashes.

The injections will continue six months,
then take more than another year to clear my system.

Implications which render both my prospects
and, fortuitously, my desire
for a resuscitated romantic life
ever more deeply dormant.

Friday morning, I awoke to find blood spots
on my sheets.

I'd been told this building was crawling with bedbugs.
I'd seen the Orkin truck so often I wondered
if we had a resident exterminator.

But no.
A quick inspection of my mattress
and an internet photo search confirmed it:
I'd been bitten.

Or smitten.
Or smote.
Whatever.

I ran all my bedding
on three-hour maximum-heat sanitizing cycles.
Bought a 2.5-gallon jug of Orkin spray at Home Depot
and emptied it.

Even baked the wooden slat supports for my mattress
(after dousing them with pesticide)
for twenty minutes at 175 degrees.
One-twenty-five kills the eggs,
but I wasn't messing around.

Throughout Friday, texts from siblings in Minnesota:
our mother had taken another downturn.
Hospice now expected her to pass that weekend
or early next week.

They offered to help with travel expenses
if I could fly immediately,
but I explained my procedures for radiation prep
scheduled Monday and Tuesday.

One brother arranged for me to say a few words
via his phone into my mother's hearing aids this morning.
He also read a poem I'd written for her and sent to him.

She was unresponsive,
but I expect our familiar voices,
expressions of love and peace,
soothed her at some level
along with the touch of those there with her:
my siblings and their families.

My relationships with both of my parents
especially my mother
have always been conflicted.

I don't feel we were ever close,
except in the way one is with hand-to-hand combatants.

But life has taught me to respect parents
as well as opponents,
even when they are one and the same.

They shape who we are.
They teach us, of necessity,
to accept and take pride in being who we are.

My parents loved me
for what they wanted me to be
an evangelist akin to Billy Graham
and were anguished that my life choices
would separate me for eternity
from the rest of the family.

A sadly unsatisfying love,
  but one they felt deeply,
  and to which they were true.
  I can respect that.

This is the poem I wrote to my mother, which one of my
brothers read to her on my behalf:

"God Is Love"

is so much larger
  than any scolding
  we may give ourselves

for things we've done
  or not done
  or not done well enough.

Love transforms
  our errors, our debts
  into credits

for lessons learned,
  for wisdom, direction
  for those who follow.

Love absolves us,
  dissolves our doubts,

bestows strength,
courage, confidence

to lift our heads,
 to relax our shoulders,
 to open our arms

to embrace, be embraced,
 to step with joy
 into joy

beyond our comprehension,
 to be at peace
 beyond ourselves.

With love, from Philip
3/31/2024

Note: I did not weep while watching my mother's funeral, nor had I while attending my father's funeral eight months prior. But neither did I scowl, taste resentment, or bitterness.

I observed, respectfully, recognizing that that they did love me, as best they were able, given who they were, given the framework they had built to shelter their own lives, given their unshakeable belief that unless I repented of loving men, I would be separated for eternity from the rest of the family, given that they both bore to their graves the heavy weight of their conviction that their son was responsible for already having directed other parents' beloved sons to eternal damnation.

Likewise, I have loved them as best I am able by attempting honestly to understand and honor their lives and the directions they inspired me to find for my own. They loved each other well and deeply, and I once referenced that love in one of my poems for Stephen: *"Let me hallow the fact of us / with honor for those who taught us how to love."*

About the Author

Philip Hughes-Luing

Having grown up on a subsistence farm in the rural backwoods of northern Minnesota, Philip Hughes-Luing's first exposure to artmaking occurred his freshman year of college as a nude model for the Art Department of Cornell College in Mt. Vernon, Iowa. A Theater and Philosophy double major, during his junior year he first enrolled in an art class. At the Art faculty's invitation, he presented a Senior Thesis show in Fine Arts his senior year.

He planned to attend art school after college until a positive HIV test required the pursuit of medical insurance. He devoted twenty hours per week for nearly forty years to creating artwork while working administrative jobs at a medical center in Chicago. He has worked with charcoal and pastels, oil and acrylic paints, and ceramics.

Following the death of a life partner in 1994, he moved into Artists in Residence, an apartment complex leasing only to writers, musicians, and visual artists while obtaining an M.A. in Interdisciplinary Arts from Columbia College of Chicago in 2000. Altogether, he has grieved the deaths of four intended life partners since the age of sixteen, serving as the primary caregiver for three. All four were visually or musically creative.

His fourth partner died in 2013. He retired from the medical center in 2015 and retired to Grants Pass, Oregon, but following a series of strokes in 2017 sold his live-in studio along a salmon stream to stay at an assisted care facility. Physically and cognitively debilitated, he was unable to hold a pen or paintbrush. His impaired mental acuity undercut his filing for disability as well, which was denied due to insufficient documentation.

Depleted, rather than filing an appeal, he donated his belongings, including forty years' worth of the artwork he'd created or collected from other artists, to a Goodwill donation center, then headed to Oregon's coast to wade away into the currents. Instead, he ended up at a homeless shelter in Eugene, Oregon, staying there for over a year composing poetry. Unable to hold a paintbrush, he used tubes of liquid paint with a "sling, splash, splatter, and drip" technique to paint on donated clothes in a public park, a collection which still constitutes most of his wardrobe. When he arrived in

Albuquerque, New Mexico in October of 2019, he had been homeless since April Fool's Day of 2018, which had coincided with Easter Sunday that year.

In November of 2019 he obtained transitional housing located a block from the OffCenter Community Arts Project, which he started attending immediately. In February of 2020 he participated in a drawing class, using jumbo-sized chalks, and by May he could again hold and manipulate a paintbrush. He acquired an easel and has spent most of his time since then in front of it. Since May of 2020 he has created well over 250 paintings with acrylics and water-soluble oils on canvases ranging in size from 18"x24" to 30"x48". Currently he serves as Treasurer on OffCenter's Board of Directors, assists with OffCenter's weekly Writing Group, and facilitates a weekly "Tell Your Story Group" at ArtStreet, a community studio situated in the Albuquerque HealthCare for the Homeless complex.

Artist's Statement

Like love, art is no one thing
 but many and varied expressions
 of our survival instinct.

I believe that creating and viewing art serves our human survival instinct by developing our intuitive abilities. Using intuition, we instantly organize information in our subconscious minds into a coherent metaphor, a "big picture" that explains the world around us, alerting us to hidden dangers or leading us to unseen opportunities.

Philosophically I align with Jackson Pollack's Jungian-inspired ideas about using spontaneity to access and express subconscious material. My creative process is to empty my mind of any conscious intention and allow myself to be drawn to select colors and brushes intuitively, in the moment. Spontaneously I make a mark, then another. My only rule is that each mark must respond somehow to the preceding mark. Allowing intuition to guide me, I dance my marks into balance with each other until I am caught by surprise when a moment of exquisite, delicate harmony between all the elements at play in the piece emerges.

At those times I pause and wait. Sometimes the moment proves fleeting, and I will resume the dance. When the piece is done, though, the moment stands still, and the piece feels at rest. Chaos and order have found balance. I feel that I have drawn from my subconscious a visual expression of an emotional state held in response to one or more of the concerns in my life, something which, whether hopeful or sad, feels expressive of our shared human existence. By doing so, I trust that my expression will find spiritual or psychological common ground with my viewers.

That is not to say that common ground is necessarily stable, unshifting ground. In our contemporary Digital Information Age, we no longer live in a time of simple, definitive statements. Instead, we contemplate complexities. Almost instantaneously, information, whether presented as fact, fiction, opinion, theory, speculation, or any combination thereof, reverberates globally from every possible angle. Too often each reflection is generally presented to us as exclusively true, yet we find that what appears accurate from one angle appears distorted from another.

Without unbiased means for reconciling all the differing perspectives that bombard us, we must learn to live comfortably with ambiguity and ambivalence if we are to maintain our sanity, peace of mind, and the ability to find joy. To be relevant and true to the times in which I live and create, with my art I search for ways to find balance and harmony, ways to maintain a sense of equilibrium within the complexities whirling around me. I hope art will help us find ways to see beyond all the confusion, ways to listen for music within and beyond the noise.

When I contemplate one of my paintings, I like to relax my gaze, which allows me to travel through time, from the front plane, through the surface drops, splatters, and runs of color, through the dancefloor of brushstrokes performing gyrations of different sizes, intensities, and attitudes, clear back to a glimpse of the beginning of the painting, the first layer of color, sometimes back to a bit of white canvas.

Traveling from front to back, there's always something happening behind where my eye is resting, something further off that's partially obscured, something that asks what's happening back there, how can I get there, and is it safe? Feeling my way through, I lose track of myself and my external world as I explore the mystery unfolding within my mind.

🌐 **www.philiphughesluing.com**

A Note of Thanks

The extensive editing and layout design services provided by Hannah Ajayi, whom I procured through Upwork, have been delicate, sophisticated, insightful, and made with great empathy. Passages with experimental syntax, spellings, etc. are at my insistence and likely against her better judgment. I am fortunate to have found an editor as flexible as she is competent and meticulously careful about letting my words speak. Ms. Ajayi designed the book cover, utilizing one of my paintings.

Prior to the compilation of this manuscript, I received valuable guidance from literary consultant Christi Craig, the Publisher of Hidden Timber Books, whose gently delivered insights taught me to winnow a regurgitation of nearly every thought I'd ever had about life into a body of raw materials fit for eventual fashioning into this memorial to four men whose memories I hold dear. I also greatly appreciate the input and assistance that I received from Mika Maloney, Mandy Gardner, Tamra Hays, and Myke Skyé, all denizens of OffCenter Community Arts in Albuquerque, New Mexico.

www.ingramcontent.com/pod-product-compliance
Lightning Source LLC
Chambersburg PA
CBHW070907130626
46555CB00001B/34